✧ *Companions for the Journey* ✧

Praying with
John Cardinal Newman

✧ *Companions for the Journey* ✧

Praying with
John Cardinal Newman

by
Halbert Weidner, CO

Saint Mary's Press
Christian Brothers Publications
Winona, Minnesota

The publishing team for this book included Rosemary Broughton, development editor; Carl Koch, series editor; Laurie A. Berg, copy editor; Lynn Dahdal, production editor and typesetter; Maurine R. Twait, art director; Kent Linder, cover designer; Elaine Kohner, illustrator; pre-press, printing, and binding by the graphics division of Saint Mary's Press.

The acknowledgments continue on page 117.

Printed in the United States of America

Printing: 9 8 7 6 5 4 3 2 1

Year: 2005 04 03 02 01 00 99 98 97

ISBN 0-88489-409-6

✧ Contents ✧

✧ Foreword ✧

Companions for the Journey

Just as food is required for human life, so are companions. Indeed, the word *companions* comes from two Latin words: *com,* meaning "with," and *panis,* meaning "bread." Companions nourish our heart, mind, soul, and body. They are also the people with whom we can celebrate the sharing of bread.

Perhaps the most touching stories in the Bible are about companionship: the Last Supper, the wedding feast at Cana, the sharing of the loaves and the fishes, and Jesus' breaking of bread with the disciples on the road to Emmaus. Each incident of companionship with Jesus revealed more about his mercy, love, wisdom, suffering, and hope. When Jesus went to pray in the Garden of Olives, he craved the companionship of the Apostles. They let him down. But God sent the Spirit to inflame the hearts of the Apostles, and they became faithful companions to Jesus and to on another.

Throughout history, other faithful companions have followed Jesus and the Apostles. These saints and mystics have also taken the journey from conversion, through suffering, to resurrection. Just as they were inspired by the holy people who went before them, so too may you take them as your companions as you walk on your spiritual journey.

The Companions for the Journey series is a response to the spiritual hunger of Christians. This series makes available the rich spiritual teachings of mystics and guides whose wisdom can help us on our pilgrimages. As you complete the last meditation in each volume, it is hoped that you will feel supported, challenged, and affirmed by a soul-companion on your spiritual journey.

The spiritual hunger that has emerged over the last twenty years is a great sign of renewal in Christian life. People fill retreat programs and workshops on topics in spirituality. The demand for spiritual directors exceeds the number available. Interest in the lives and writings of saints and mystics is increasing as people search for models of whole and holy Christian life.

Praying with Newman

Praying with Frederic Ozanam is more than just a book about Newman's spirituality. This book seeks to engage you in praying in the way that Newman did about issues and themes that were central to his experience. Each meditation can enlighten your understanding of his spirituality and lead you to reflect on your own experience.

The goal of *Praying with John Cardinal Newman* is that you will discover Newman's rich spirituality and integrate his spirit and wisdom into your relationship with God, with your brothers and sisters, and with your own heart and mind.

Suggestions for Praying with Newman

Meet John Cardinal Newman, a fascinating companion for your pilgrimage, by reading the introduction to this book. It provides a brief biography of Newman and an outline of the major themes of his spirituality.

Once you meet Newman, you will be ready to pray with him and to encounter God, your sisters and brothers, and yourself in new and wonderful ways. To help your prayer, here are some suggestions that have been part of the Tradition of Christian spirituality:

Create a sacred space. Jesus said, "When you pray, go to your room, shut yourself in, and so pray to your [God] who is in that secret place, and your [God] who sees all that is done in secret will reward you" (Matthew 6:6). Solitary prayer is best done in a place where you can have privacy and silence, both of which can be luxuries in the life of busy people. If privacy and silence are not possible, create a quiet, safe place within yourself, perhaps while riding to and from work, while sitting in line at the dentist's office, or while waiting for someone. Do the best you can, knowing that a loving God is present everywhere. Whether the meditations in this book are used for solitary prayer or with a group, try to create a prayerful mood with candles, meditative music, an open Bible, or a crucifix.

Open yourself to the power of prayer. Every human experience has a religious dimension. All of life is suffused with God's presence. So remind yourself that God is present as you begin your period of prayer. Do not worry about distractions. If something keeps intruding during your prayer, spend some time talking with God about it. Be flexible because God's Spirit blows where it will.

Prayer can open your mind and widen your vision. Be open to new ways of seeing God, people, and yourself. As you open yourself to the Spirit of God, different emotions are evoked, such as sadness from tender memories, or joy from a celebration recalled. Our emotions are messages from God that can tell us much about our spiritual quest. Also, prayer strengthens our will to act. Through prayer, God can touch our will and empower us to live according to what we know is true.

Finally, many of the meditations in this book will call you to employ your memories, your imagination, and the circumstances of your life as subjects for prayer. The great mystics and saints realized that they had to use all their resources to know God better. Indeed, God speaks to us continually and touches us constantly. We must learn to listen and feel with all the means that God has given us.

Come to prayer with an open mind, heart, and will.

Preview each meditation before beginning. After you have placed yourself in God's presence, spend a few moments previewing the readings and especially the reflection activities. Several reflection activities are given in each meditation because different styles of prayer appeal to different personalities or personal needs. **Note that each meditation has more reflection activities than can be done during one prayer period.**

Therefore, select only one or two reflection activities each time you use a meditation. Do not feel compelled to complete all the reflection activities.

Read meditatively. Each meditation offers you a story about Frederic and a reading from his writings. Take your time reading. If a particular phrase touches you, stay with it. Relish its feelings, meanings, and concerns.

Use the reflections. Following the readings is a short reflection in commentary form, which is meant to give perspective to the readings. Then you are offered several ways of meditating on the readings and the theme of the prayer. You may be familiar with the different methods of meditating, but in case you are not, they are described briefly here:

✦ *Repeated short prayer or mantra*: One means of focusing your prayer is to use a *mantra,* or "prayer word." The mantra may be a single word or a short phrase taken from the readings or from the Scriptures. For example, the short prayer for meditation 2 in this book is "Lead, Kindly, Light." Repeated slowly in harmony with your breathing, the mantra helps you center your heart and mind on one action or attribute of God.

✦ *Lectio divina*: This type of meditation is "divine studying," a concentrated reflection on the word of God or the wisdom of a spiritual writer. Most often in *lectio divina*, you will be invited to read one of the passages several times and then concentrate on one or two sentences, pondering their meaning for you and their effect on you. *Lectio divina* commonly ends with formulation of a resolution.

✦ *Guided meditation*: In this type of meditation, our imagination helps us consider alternative actions and likely consequences. Our imagination helps us experience new ways of seeing God, our neighbors, ourselves, and nature. When Jesus told his followers parables and stories, he engaged their imagination. In this book, you will be invited to follow guided meditations.

One way of doing a guided meditation is to read the scene or story several times, until you know the outline and can recall it when you enter into reflection. Or before your prayer time, you may wish to record the meditation on a tape recorder. If so, remember to allow pauses for reflection between phrases and to speak with a slow, peaceful pace and tone. Then, during prayer, when you have finished the readings and the reflection commentary, you can turn on your recording of the meditation and be led through it. If you find your own voice too distracting, ask a friend to make the tape for you.

✦ *Examen of consciousness*: The reflections often will ask you to examine how God has been speaking to you in your past and present experience—in other words, the reflections will ask you to examine your awareness of God's presence in your life.

✦ *Journal writing*: Writing is a process of discovery. If you write for any length of time, stating honestly what is on your mind and in your heart, you will unearth much about who you are, how you stand with your God, what deep longings reside in your soul, and more. In some reflections, you will be asked to write a dialog with Jesus or someone else. If you have never used writing as a means of meditation, try it. Reserve a special notebook for your journal writing. If desired, you can go back to your entries at a future time for an examen of consciousness.

✦ *Action*: Occasionally, a reflection will suggest singing a favorite hymn, going out for a walk, or undertaking some other physical activity. Actions can be meaningful forms of prayer.

Using the Meditations for Group Prayer

If you wish to use the meditations for community prayer, these suggestions may help:

✦ Read the theme to the group. Call the community into the presence of God, using the short opening prayer. Invite one or two participants to read one or both readings. If you use both readings, observe the pause between them.

✦ The reflection commentary may be used as a reading, or it can be deleted, depending on the needs and interests of the group.

✦ Select one of the reflection activities for your group. Allow sufficient time for your group to reflect, to recite a centering prayer or mantra, to accomplish a studying prayer *(lectio divina)*, or to finish an examen of consciousness. Depending on the group and the amount of available time, you may want to invite the participants to share their reflections, responses, or petitions with the group.

✦ Reading the passage from the Scriptures may serve as a summary of the meditation.

✦ If a formulated prayer or a psalm is given as a closing, it may be recited by the entire group. Or you may ask participants to offer their own prayers for the closing.

Now you are ready to begin praying with John Cardinal Newman, a faithful and caring companion on this stage of your spiritual journey. It is hoped that you will find him to be a true soul-companion.

CARL KOCH
Editor

✧ Introduction ✧

Light of Vatican Council II

John Henry Newman, later Cardinal Newman, was a busy pastor, a prodigious writer, and so far ahead of his time in the nineteenth century that he has been called one of the Fathers of the Second Vatican Council. But he was best known in his own time as a spiritual friend, and his letters will soon fill more than thirty volumes. One of Newman's biographers said of him that modern people would find two very attractive features in Newman: emotional honesty and intellectual integrity.

A passion for the mystery of God and for the life of the mind, transformed Newman and made him an attractive and wise friend. Fortunately for us, friendship in his time had to be maintained mostly by writing and Newman was as gifted a writer as he was a loyal and loving friend.

The many written works that he left after his ninety years, recording his struggle with the issues of the church in his day, are still a rich resource for Christians today. They have already been reflected in the fruition of Vatican Council II and the documents promulgated after each session.

Newman's Childhood

Newman was born on 21 February 1801, and was named after his father. Within ten years, five other Newman children were born: Charles, Harriet, Francis, Jemima, and Mary. Newman's father, an Englishman, was a partner in a banking firm. His mother, Jemima Fourdrinier, came from a Protestant family who had immigrated from France.

13

Newman recalled receiving, at five years of age, his first letter from his father. His father encouraged him, a young boy who could already read, to study his multiplication table and his pence table, and promised the gift of a copy-book upon his return. Later in his life, Newman noted that he always thought better with a paper and pen at hand; he even remarked that the quality of the pen influenced the level of work he was able to do.

His father's bank ran into serious difficulty when Newman was an adolescent, and the whole family was concerned about settling accounts, paying creditors, and keeping their good name. John's mother was especially concerned about John's reaction to this situation. She wrote to her sister, "I have just written to Dr. Nicholas [at John's school], and asked for dear John to come for a day or two. I think it will be a great relief to him and us to talk it over. I am anxious to know how the dear fellow feels, and I trust to be able to soften any keen feelings he may have" (Maisie Ward, *Young Mr. Newman*, p. 19). His mother recognized John's sensitivity to people, a sensitivity that is reflected in the motto he chose for himself on becoming cardinal many years later: *Cor ad cor loquitur*—Heart speaks to heart.

London Evangelical

Newman was born in London and within the Church of England. His first great religious experience was as an Evangelical Anglican. What did it mean to be both Anglican and Evangelical?

The Church of England was and is an "established," or state, church. To be born English is to have a claim on the church. But all state denominations—Protestant, Anglican, Catholic—suffer from this kind of official status. A combination of church and state invites people motivated by politics and power to become authorities in relation to a faith that invites people to the cross and to service. The Church of England had great saints, as did other established churches, but there was a lot of confusion between the demands of the gospel and the demands of polite society. Even more unfortunate in Newman's time were the attempts to ignore or minimize the Christian creed so that the church could command the widest possible acceptance among the citizenry. The church's teachings became a kind of negotiable platform subject to committee and convention.

One of the reactions to this situation came from within the church. Evangelical Anglicans stressed a "born-again" religious conversion that guaranteed a salvation that infant baptism—viewed by them as formal ritual—could not accomplish. The rite of baptism was often so formal that it seemed to be more a social rite of passage than a giving of the Holy Spirit in Christ.

In this religious context, as a schoolboy under Evangelical headmaster Walter Mayers, Newman felt that he had had an encounter with Christ that was real and that changed him. He was then fifteen years old.

But fifteen years old in 1816 was already adulthood for the farmer or factory worker. For the middle class it was the final year of preparatory school before university. Newman was born just a few years after the French Revolution, which had attacked church and crown with the weapon of reason and the books of philosophers. Newman was reading these philosophers and could have gone in that direction as did one of his brothers. Instead, he turned to a religion of experience and of the heart and did so without negating a brilliant mind. For the rest of his life, Newman would never abandon the combination of religious experience and reason. He retained a profound belief in the necessity of both doctrine and conversion. Religious experience needed to be reinforced by doctrine, the product of thinking. Doctrine safeguarded the validity of religious experience. To receive doctrine was to be addressed by God within a relationship of profound love. Newman declared, "Persons influence us, voices melt us, looks subdue us, deeds inflame us. Many a man will live and die upon a dogma: no man will be a martyr for a conclusion" (John Henry Cardinal Newman, *Discussions and Arguments on Various Subjects*, p. 293). Revelation was for Newman a personal and direct address, a way of being grasped by God in such a way that our whole person moves to respond. Newman did not get a chance to die for truth, but his whole life was an opportunity to live for it.

Upon the death of Walter Mayers, headmaster and then later "great friend," Newman would say:

> "Whatever religious feeling I have within me, to his kind instructions when I was at school I am especially indebted for it—and it may (I think) be safely said, that had it not been for my intimacy with him, I should not have possessed the comfort of that knowledge of God which (poor as it is) enabled me to go through the dangerous season of my Undergraduate residence" (Ian Ker and Thomas Gornall, eds., *Letters and Diaries of John Henry Newman*, II, p. 58)

Later, as a Catholic, Newman remembered the anniversary of Mayer's death every year.

Oxford Failure and Success

In these days of SAT scores, Graduate Record Exams, entrance tests to law and medical schools, it is hard to believe that there was an era when a gentleman's son simply went off to university without application or test scores. A few months short of his seventeenth birthday, Newman enrolled in Oxford University. The family had not been able to decide whether he should go to Cambridge University or to Oxford, and the carriage was actually waiting when a friend of the family showed up and convinced John's father to enroll John at Oxford. It was simply a matter of finding a vacancy in one of the better colleges in the university.

The town of Oxford has a collection of old and new colleges, each with its own name and history, which make up the federation that is the university. Some tourists get very frustrated after looking at some of the colleges because they have come to Oxford to see the "University," but there is none to see! Even stranger, there are no classes. Tutors help students study and write essays. Faculty offer lectures, but no exams are given in these lectures. Within a three-year period a series of exams is given, with the final exams at the end graded: fail, pass, seconds, upper seconds, and firsts.

While Newman relished such independence in study, the lack of a distinct curriculum led him to exhaust himself by going in all directions. So he did poorly in the final examinations. He took a second in classics and failed altogether in mathematics. His life in the university should have been over. He was just short of his twentieth birthday.

However, Newman had done very well in preliminary exams and he had obtained a scholarship that allowed him to stay on for a few more years of study. A year later his thoughts turned to teaching and to ordination, which was required of all teaching fellows at the university. At the same time, he decided to stand for another examination. This time the prize was a teaching fellowship at the leading college of the time, Oriel, which was pioneering an intellectual revolution in quality of fellows and students. The exams lasted five days with essays in English and Latin, a journal article to be translated into Latin, twelve essay questions on philosophy

and mathematics, ten on logic, with nine books as subjects for an oral examination. The usual winners were students who had graduated with firsts in both their chosen subjects.

But Oriel was looking for original minds, and Newman's was not only original, this time it was also clear. Much to Newman's surprise, he won the fellowship and embarked on a remarkable career as educator and pastor. In his day, fellows did not marry, so anyone who made a life's work of education, and this was rare, accepted a real vocation. He intended to embrace celibacy, live and die as a Fellow of Oriel. Whether as tutor or as pastor, Newman felt to his dying day that both his fellowship and his ordination gave him the responsibility for souls.

Besides "souls," Newman also had responsibility for his family. His father died in 1824, after barely surviving one of the economic busts of the prior decade. This left Newman as the economic mainstay for his mother, two brothers, and three sisters. The family suffered another loss when his sister Mary died suddenly a few years later. Newman always kept her death anniversary and remembered her death as a major event in his own faith journey.

During this time Newman gradually moved toward a *via media*, or middle way, that held that the Church of England was not to be a form of Protestantism but a part of the Church Catholic, which was both reformed and anti-Roman. This move cost him one of his roles as an educator when the provost of his college, fearing religious influence, refused to assign him any more students to be tutored. Newman had not, in fact, discussed religion during tutorials, but his popularity with the undergraduates made him more influential than the prevailing powers wanted.

Fortunately for Newman, he already had a bully pulpit that was in fact a real pulpit: before the rift with the provost, he had been appointed rector of the University Church of Saint Mary's. He was never an Anglican ritualist, following Catholic rites, but he did implement all the services possible using the *Anglican Book of Common Prayer*. The six volumes of his sermons, *Parochial and Plain Sermons*, are classics of teaching and experiential religion. They were given in a nonemotional manner and were all the more powerful for that. They remain in print today and are used by Protestants and Catholics.

Newman became a preacher so popular with university students and so disliked by officials that college schedules were arranged to conflict with Sunday evensong, forcing undergraduates to choose between meals and listening to his sermons. Alarmed at his sway, college authorities tried to thwart Newman.

Because of his schedule and the ongoing conflict with Oxford authorities, in 1833, an exhausted Newman left with friends for a journey to classical Italy and Sicily. They intended to avoid Roman Catholicism as much as possible. At the end of the journey Newman fell desperately ill, and on recovering composed the poem "The Pillar of the Cloud." The poem celebrates the inner guidance that Newman relied on and his intuition that a crisis was coming that would require great faith:

> Lead, Kindly Light, amid the encircling gloom,
> > Lead Thou me on!
> The night is dark, and I am far from home—
> > Lead Thou me on!
> Keep Thou my feet; I do not ask to see
> > The distant scene,—one step enough for me.
> > (Geoffrey Tillotson, comp., *Newman: Prose and Poetry*,
> > p. 807)

The Oxford Movement

On his return to England, Newman confronted the crisis that was brewing in the Church of England over Parliament's control of its affairs. Newman and his friends joined a loosely organized movement that began to make formal demands for the spiritual renewal of the Church of England and to call it back to its Catholic roots. Not wanting to reform and renew by committee, the leaders published a series of "Tracts for the Times" out of a general agreement on principles, but leaving each writer free as to the details and the style.

Newman's was the first tract issued in what became known as the Oxford Movement. In it he called on the rather gentlemanly and restrained Anglican bishops to prepare for martyrdom if that were necessary to obtain the recognition of their authority as successors of the Apostles rather than as merely officers of the state and members of the House of Lords. He writes pointedly, "We could not wish them [the bishops] a more blessed termination of their course, than the spoiling of their goods, and martyrdom" (Ward, *Young Mr. Newman,* p. 249).

Needless to say, this was not a termination for which any of them devoutly or otherwise wished. But Newman's imagination would always be colored by the evangelical zeal of the early church, and the martyrs seemed to fulfill the exact role model needed to show England that the movement was serious and that reform was necessary.

But the movement wanted to appeal to more than the bishops. In a book on the early church, Newman had written that the bishops of the Church Catholic even then could be timid and uncertain. During the Arian controversy, the laity held for Jesus as God and man while the bishops wavered. So in the second tract, Newman called on the laity to preserve Catholic orthodoxy in the Church of England. Later as a Roman Catholic, he would return to this theme of the laity being preserved in their faith by the Holy Spirit and the importance for the bishops to consult the faithful.

The Move to Rome

As it turned out, the leaders of the Oxford Movement were more likely to be the martyrs if the general public and the political powers had their way. Politics muddied the waters considerably because the Oxford Movement seemed to be against reform of Parliament that up to then had excluded Roman Catholics and dissenting non-Anglican Protestants like Quakers and Methodists. But the Church of England was subject to Parliament, and if non-Anglicans were allowed into Parliament, the church would be subject to those outside of its membership. Eventually, Newman and a number of others saw that state establishment of the Church of England would probably have to go if real reform of the Church of England were to take place.

Newman's position proved difficult. He had to argue against Protestants within his own church who thought him too Roman Catholic. He also struggled against Roman Catholics who thought his ideas about Anglicanism were unreal and disguised a church which was basically Protestant and not at all Catholic.

Under this heavy opposition, Newman moved out of Oriel College to lodgings renovated from old stables in Littlemore, just outside of Oxford. Littlemore became Newman's place to think and to pray. He took direct care of a small parish church nearby that was under his direction as rector of Saint Mary's. A small community of friends formed around him. They committed themselves to a heavy schedule of prayer, silence, fasting, and study. They wore no special garb and still followed the *Anglican Book of Common Prayer,* but they were accused of "monkishness."

A few years earlier, Newman had written in a letter about Roman Catholic missionaries in England:

> If they want to convert England, let them go barefoot into our manufacturing towns—let them preach to the people like St. Francis Xavier—let them be pelted and trampled on—and I will admit that they can do what we cannot. . . . Let them use the proper arms of the Church, and they will prove that they are the Church by using them. (Meriol Trevor, *Newman: The Pillar of the Cloud,* p. 252)

It would be just such a barefooted friar, the Passionist Father Dominic Barberi, who would receive Newman and several of his friends into full communion with the Church of Rome.

By 1845, after twelve years of trying to maintain the Catholicity of the Anglican church against Anglican authority itself, Newman departed. This had been a terrible struggle. He knew that if the Church of England was not Catholic, that did not necessarily make the Church of Rome the right place either. Both denominations could be wrong!

His dilemma was that neither the Church of England nor the Church of Rome actually looked like the early church. If the Church of England were politicized, the Church of Rome was itself a political entity, with the pope not only Bishop of Rome but head of a large territory, the Papal States. Further, while the other territories of Italy were uniting as one nation, the pope was resisting vigorously. The Papal States were believed to be a fundamental necessity to the Roman Catholic church.

If both the Anglican and Roman churches were so politicized, where should Newman go? How could he tell which, if either, was Catholic? Which was the "one, holy, catholic, and apostolic church" of the creed?

As an answer, Newman began to write an essay on the question of the development of doctrine. The very idea was a horror to most orthodox Christians, Protestant or Catholic. Orthodoxy was popularly defined as Christian beliefs that had never changed, and development was a kind of change. Adding fuel to the controversy of Newman's position, Quakers, Unitarians, and other liberal denominations accused the mainline churches of having added to, changed, and distorted the original simplicity of Christ's teachings. Was Newman agreeing with the Quakers and Unitarians? It seemed so.

But Newman thought not. If Anglicans believed that Catholic ideas about the pope were not there originally, Newman thought they also had to admit the same thing about such doctrines of the Trinity. Revelation was given the church by Jesus, but it would take centuries to truly understand what was implicit in the doctrines. New questions, new cultures, new languages emerge, and so answers must be developed that are true to the original revelation, but deeper and more varied to suit the new situation.

Newman came to accept that the modern teachings of the Roman church were Catholic in their roots and in their meanings. Those teachings had, by necessity and under the Holy Spirit, developed to meet the new challenges of being a universal church in and through time. If it was the nature of doctrine to develop, there needed to be a gift of the Spirit given to prevent falsity or error in faith and an authoritative body that could decide, after long debate and consideration, what were authentic developments of the truth of revelation.

Newman reasoned that the gift of infallibility given to the church by Christ and the Spirit was manifested in the role and function of the pope and the bishops within the church in relation to the "deposit of faith." This deposit of faith was not simply handed down and preserved by passive transmission, as Newman had thought originally. It was a living teaching, a living Tradition, that carried the mystery of God's revelation.

After Newman came into the Church of Rome on 9 October 1845, some Catholics were horrified on reading *An Essay on the Development of Christian Doctrine*. Newman simply replied that he was now a Catholic even if he had come in for the wrong reason. Since the book was written by the Anglican Newman, the Catholic Newman did not have to answer for it. Since his time it has become a standard for Catholics, while the idea of development of doctrine is acceptable to nearly all denominations.

Newman later reflected that in coming into communion with the Church of Rome:

> I was not conscious to myself, on my conversion, of any change, intellectual or moral, wrought in my mind. I was not conscious of firmer faith in the fundamental truths of Revelation, or of more self-command; I had not more fervour; but it was like coming into port after a rough sea; and my happiness on that score remains to this day without interruption. (John Henry Cardinal Newman, *Apologia Pro Vita Sua*, p. 238)

The Oratory

When Newman was looking for a home in the Catholic church, he was led to a congregation of secular priests and laymen known as the Oratory of Saint Philip Neri. An oratory is a place to pray, not to orate. The original Oratory was simply the prayer room where Philip Neri had gathered his disciples. Philip had lived in the 1500s and had become known as the second apostle of Rome. He had wanted to go off to the Indies like Francis Xavier, but a visionary monk had told him that Rome was to be his Indies and that his mission was to make Catholics out of Catholics.

Philip's movement originally consisted entirely of laity, but gradually he and others were ordained to serve the lay movement that gathered around him for afternoon prayer meetings and in the evening for meditation. He insisted on the secular nature of the community and would allow no vows, oaths, or promises. The primitive church ideal of the Book of Acts was sufficient. Philip was extraordinarily cheerful, mystical, and practical, so the Oratory began to thrive even when Roman authorities were afraid it was a Protestant sect because there was so much Bible reading and lay preaching.

The Catholic bishop of Birmingham, Nicholas Wiseman, befriended Newman and suggested the Oratory. Newman and his friends who had joined him saw the Oratory as a feasible way to maintain community, prayer, and ministry without a lot of structure. Newman spent the rest of his life as an Oratorian in Birmingham, even when Wiseman had become cardinal archbishop in London and a new oratory was started there too.

Seasons of Darkness

Newman would say that while he was an Anglican his religion had been difficult, but his life exciting. As a Roman Catholic his religion had been exciting, but his life difficult. If as an Anglican he had been suspected of being a Roman Catholic, as a Catholic he was held to be dangerously half-baked and rather Protestant. His life as a Catholic consisted mostly of works attempted and frustrated.

Around 1854, Newman was asked to found the position of and become the first rector of the Catholic University of Ireland. This job required dividing his time and presence between Birmingham, England and Dublin, Ireland. He was assured that he would become a bishop so that the university rectorship would carry authority. Then nothing was said again.

The Irish bishops wanted a quasi-seminary. Newman the Oxonian wanted a real university with significant lay administration. Stonewalled, Newman eventually resigned.

Next, Newman was asked by his bishop to found an oratory in Oxford itself. Rome gave permission only if Newman himself would not go there. The bishops proposed Newman as a translator of the Bible so that English Catholics might have a version as eloquent as the King James Version, but the church authorities let the project lapse.

Perhaps the most difficult of Newman's challenges came from a request to defend the honor of the church. An ex-priest from Italy was attacking the Catholic church; Cardinal Wiseman asked Newman to publicly respond, assuring him that he had plenty of evidence on the priest's sexual misconduct. When the man sued Newman, Wiseman could not produce all the proper evidence and the prejudice of the judge prevented the admission of much that was available. Newman lost the case and could have faced prison. Loyal initiatives and subsequent failures marked his life for twenty years.

Writing Out of Frustration

Two wonderful books came out of such frustrations. The first was *The Idea of a University,* originally lectures Newman gave in Dublin that articulated a vision of education. The second was his *Apologia Pro Vita Sua,* or defense of his life.

The attack this time had come from a very respectable Protestant source, Charles Kingsley, a chaplain to Queen Victoria and a popular writer. He had accused Newman of lying about his religious stance while an Anglican and in general accused Catholic clergy of being careless of the truth since they had to defend Rome at all costs.

The *Apologia* covered the Anglican period of Newman's life. The effort of gathering materials and letters reunited him with many former colleagues in the Church of England who rallied to defend his honor and reactivate their friendship with him. It restored Newman to his place in the English national consciousness, but did not help him with either the Anglican or the Roman Catholic hierarchy who still suspected him.

Newman's Conscience

His conscience had led Newman to the Church of Rome, and the same conscience perplexed and infuriated some Roman Catholics. While being loyal to the church and always at its service, Newman faced several controversies.

First, the idea of development of doctrine, fairly original with Newman, took a long time to prevail within the mainstream of the church. Later, advocates of Marian doctrines and papal authority, even some extremists in these matters, would take up the idea of development as a way to justify teachings that were not explicit in the early church.

Second, there was the matter of an article Newman wrote entitled "Consulting the Faithful in Matters of Doctrine." After the early church Council of Nicaea that produced the Nicene Creed, Newman noted that:

> The episcopate . . . did not, as a class or order of men, play a good part in the troubles consequent on the Council; and the laity did. The Catholic people, in the length and breadth of Christendom, were the obstinate champions of Catholic truth, and the bishops were not. (John Henry Cardinal Newman, *Arians of the Fourth Century*, p. 445)

Therefore, Newman believed that it was appropriate for the bishops, before making up their minds about a matter of teaching, to consult the living faith of the laity.

The pope had, as a matter of fact, done that before the proclamation of the Immaculate Conception. Nevertheless, a furor erupted over Newman's historically embarrassing facts and practical suggestions about the laity. Newman was reported to Rome for heresy, and because the charges were never passed on to him as they should have been, the Roman authorities took his subsequent silence as dangerous arrogance.

Third, there was Newman's moderate approach to the pastoral application of authority. He accepted the authority of the pope. Nevertheless, he believed that it was historically accurate to say that restraint on the pope's part was the most helpful feature of the power of the office:

> There never was a time when the intellect of the educated class was more active, or rather more restless, than in the middle ages. And then again all through Church history from the first, how slow is authority in interfering! Perhaps a local teacher, or a doctor in some local school, hazards a proposition, and a controversy ensues. It smoulders or burns in one place, no one interposing; Rome simply

lets it alone. Then it comes before a Bishop; or some priest, or some professor in some other seat of learning takes it up; and then there is a second stage of it. Then it comes before a University, and it may be condemned by the theological faculty. So the controversy proceeds year after year, and Rome is still silent. . . . Many a man has ideas, which he hopes are true, and useful for his day, but he is not confident about them, and wishes to have them discussed. He is willing, or rather would be thankful, to give them up, if they can be proved to be erroneous or dangerous, and by means of controversy he obtains his end. He is answered, and he yields; or on the contrary he finds that he is considered safe. He would not dare to do this, if he knew an authority, which was supreme and final, was watching every word he said, and made signs of assent or dissent to each sentence, as he uttered it . . . by reason of the very power of the Popes they have commonly been slow and moderate in their use of it. (Newman, *Apologia*, pp. 266–268)

Last, Newman could not see a conflict between conscience and authority because divine authority is manifested both in church authority and in the conscience of believers. To destroy conscience and its prerogatives would be to destroy the basis of the church itself. When the doctrine of papal infallibility was proclaimed in 1870, at Vatican Council I, extremists in regard to the papal role took advantage of the fact that the council had been interrupted by the armies unifying all of Italy under a secular government. These extremists emphasized the authority of the pope alone, alarming Protestants and moderate Catholics. Newman defended both the pope and a moderate interpretation of the council. In a public letter to William Gladstone, the prime minister of England, Newman explained the necessity of preserving conscience and the limits of papal infallibility in both the ecclesial and political arena. His conclusion became well known: "If I am obliged to bring religion into after-dinner toasts, (which indeed does not seem quite the thing) I shall drink—to the Pope, if you please,—still, to Conscience first, and to the Pope afterwards" (John Henry Cardinal Newman, *Certain Difficulties Felt by Anglicans in Catholic Teaching*, II, p. 261).

Newman's moderate interpretation of papal infallibility carried the day, but he paid a price. Cardinal Manning, Wiseman's successor in London, held a more extreme position, and he tried very hard to frustrate Newman as much as possible.

The Red Hat

Newman labored away in Birmingham at the Oratory school, the parish, and at his writing, all the while being more or less put aside by church authorities. Then in 1878, Pius IX died, and the new pope, Leo XIII, early the next year made Newman his first cardinal. This happened despite Cardinal Manning's opposition. Newman was allowed to remain a simple priest in the Oratory of Birmingham, but with the addition of the red hat and the honors of the new pope. Newman was seventy-eight years old!

As a cardinal, Newman was required by church law to have a private chapel, so he moved bookcases over and made a chapel behind them in his room at the Oratory. The altar was hung in the corner and on the wall to the right Newman hung the pictures of his friends, Anglican and Catholic. Once an English Oratorian was asked if this was an unusual arrangement. He responded, "Quite!" But Newman's heart still spoke to the hearts of his friends, especially in the Eucharist, and so it seemed a happy thing to have their pictures beside him at Mass.

From Shadows to Light

Newman continued to write until he was in his eighties, but he gradually weakened. He died in a simple room at the Oratory on 11 August 1890, at the age of eighty-nine. When he had been made a cardinal, his sister brought her grandson to visit. "'Which is greater,'" [the boy asked,] "'a Cardinal or a Saint?'" [Newman's] reply was, "'Cardinals belong to this world, and Saints to heaven'" (Louis Bouyer, *Newman: His Life and Spirituality*, p. 387). Many believe that this cardinal was also a saint.

He is buried in the same grave as Ambrose St. John, the one Oxonian who joined the Oratory with Newman and remained for life. Newman chose for his memorial tablet a Latin motto that translated reads: "Out of the shadows and images into the light."

Praying with Cardinal Newman

The spirituality of Newman challenges and encourages us because of characteristics that emerge from a Christianity faithfully rooted in past tradition, lived in the belief that God's revelations are constant, and looking forward in faith to a providential future and eternal joy.

Apprehending the Mystery of God

Newman laid hold of that which first laid hold of him, the Mystery of God. In his searching, in his openness to conversion, in his willingness to act for the good of the church, in his struggles with others within the ecclesiastical structures, in his hidden emotional suffering, in his extensive study and writings, Newman reflected a life founded on belief in the mystery of revelation and the Incarnation of the Word. Thus, human life for Newman could be lived at once as a great adventure and as a call to that which is divinely possible in the reality of faith.

Acting Upon the Light

The life of the mind for Newman was not for its own sake, but for the sake of truth and for action. Newman sought the light, and like the dawn, allowed it to come gradually. In waiting for the light, he learned patience and obedience. When his reason was enlightened and his convictions formed, he acted without hesitation, even while recognizing the risks involved. Newman serves as a model for acting upon the light that is given to us.

The Presence of Christ in the Spirit

Christ present within the believer as a gift of the Spirit was real to Newman. His acceptance of Trinitarian doctrine and his embrace of the Scriptures model a life based on the richest resources of the Christian Tradition.

Emotional Honesty and Intellectual Integrity

Newman lived a long time and was remarkably faithful to his friends, even when he and they were divided over serious questions of faith and loyalty. He accepted affection and gave it. He remained loyal even in discouraging circumstances. He struggled with what is important in human life while maintaining the integrity of his conscience.

Moderation in Complexity

Newman loved the church and gave his whole life to it. He often took a moderate stance in the midst of complex issues because he believed that God works gradually. Newman saw his role as a public one when addressing complex issues such as doctrinal development, the nature of the church, the identity of a Catholic university, or papal authority. He was careful and clear in his writings. For those who met him face-to-face, he appeared serene and tactful.

Newman and Our Time

Although Newman died over a hundred years ago, many believe that he is still ahead of us, and that he will be important for theology and religious thinking well into the next century. But for most people, Newman is a significant figure because he was and is a spiritual friend who was moderate and tender toward others in the midst of the complexities of life. By the example of his life, he encourages the search for God and the discipline that search requires, and he acknowledges the freedom that the children of God, in good conscience, enjoy. From him to us, *Cor ad cor loquitur*—Heart speaks to heart.

✧ Meditation 1 ✧

Holiness
Rather Than Peace

Theme: Newman discovered throughout his life that the call to holiness was contrary to accommodating himself to societal expectations. Holiness demanded more.

Opening prayer: Dear God, let me realize that my life and my world have been touched by your holiness. Let me become holy. Let me live out your saving call.

About Newman

As a young preparatory student, Newman was given an autobiography by Thomas Scott called *The Force of Truth*. Scott was a poor farmworker who had studied very hard so he could enter the clergy and enjoy economic security and social prestige. In time, Scott converted to a very disciplined spiritual life. Newman said that, humanly speaking, he almost owed his soul to Scott. Newman wrote:

> What, I suppose will strike any reader of Scott's history and writings, is his bold unworldliness and vigorous independence of mind. He followed truth wherever it led him, beginning with Unitarianism, and ending in a zealous faith

in the Holy Trinity. It was he who first planted deep in my mind that fundamental truth of religion. (Newman, *Apologia*, pp. 4–5)

Scott's mottoes became very important to Newman. One was "Holiness rather than peace," and another, "Growth—the only evidence of life."

Desire for holiness in Newman's life manifested itself in the search for the church that was one, holy, catholic, and apostolic. It showed itself in fidelity to conscience, and to the gradualness of forming intellectual convictions in relation to a living faith. After his conversion in 1845, holiness meant a way of life in both public and private acts that was consonant with his own experienced call to holiness. Over the years, Newman was a pastor, educator, scholar, community-friend, and writer.

When Newman traces his own growth in faith, he recalls that at the age of fifteen a great change took place. He became conscious of an inward conversion "of which I still am more certain than that I have hands and feet," a conviction that "would last into the next life"; he knew that he "was elected to eternal glory" (Newman, *Apologia*, pp. 3–4).

Shortly after, he speaks of another deep understanding that took possession of him around the same time, namely, that

> it would be the will of God that I should lead a single life. . . . This anticipation, which has held its ground almost continuously ever since, . . . was more or less connected in my mind with the notion, that my calling in life would require such a sacrifice as celibacy involved; as, for instance, missionary work among the heathen, to which I had a great drawing for some years. (Newman, *Apologia*, pp. 6–7)

For Newman, celibacy was a gift just as Christian revelation was a gift. Even though his commitment to celibacy placed him outside the norm, he could not accept it or other Christian beliefs without a total response of his self; both revelation and celibacy engaged the truth of his whole being.

Newman, though, did not give up wanting to love and be loved. His capacity for friendship blossomed so that both men and women felt his ability to sympathize with them. His correspondence with such women as Maria Giberne or Emily Dowles and his friendship with his married friends, John Keble and Edward Pusey, manifest Newman's deep affection and loyalty to people. Celibacy, for Newman, did not mean coldness or distance, but another way to love. It found the fullest and most stable expression in the Oratorian community in Birmingham, in the second half of Newman's life.

Pause: In the church's liturgy, the assembled people sing "Holy, holy, holy." What does this acclamation awaken in you?

Newman's Words

In a Christmas sermon at Oxford, Newman startled the hearers with his assessment of Christianity as lived out in a local congregation:

> [Christians (both penitents and the upright)] have common ground; and as they have one faith and hope, and one Spirit, so also they have one and the same circle of temptations, and one and the same confession.
>
> It were well if we understood all this. Perhaps the reason why the standard of holiness among us is so low, why our attainments are so poor, our view of the truth so dim, our belief so unreal, our general notions so artificial and external is this, that we dare not trust each other with the secret of our hearts. We have each the same secret, and we keep it to ourselves, and we fear that, as a cause of estrangement, which really would be a bond of union. We do not probe the wounds of our nature thoroughly; we do not lay the foundation of our religious profession in the ground of our inner man; we make clean the outside of things; we are amiable and friendly to each other in words and deeds, but our love is not enlarged, our bowels of affection are straitened, and we fear to let the intercourse begin at the root; and, in consequence, our religion, viewed as a social system, is hollow. The presence of Christ is not in it. (John Henry Newman, *Parochial and Plain Sermons*, V, pp. 126–127)

Reflection

Everyone, an intellectual like Newman or not, is tempted to make peace and to fit in, keeping beliefs private and passive. It makes our religion theoretically true, but practically false. As Newman warns, the presence of Christ may not be in it!

Newman suggests that a major reason for being so private and isolated from each other is an embarrassment over our spiritual hunger for God and the desire to not appear pious or holy. This social desire to fit in and to remain amiably inconspicuous may even lead us to neglect the works of mercy we know we are called to do.

In his younger days, Newman experienced the malaise in the English church, a church that was politically established and united to the government of the land. This type of civil religion allowed for the pieties of God and country as long as the gospel message and the calls to holiness were not interpreted as requiring a new public stance or experienced as too demanding. However, holiness may not always be polite.

✧ Reread the excerpt from Newman's sermon. How accurate is his diagnosis for your life of faith today? For your parish life today? Journal about your reactions to this reading, and share your thoughts with two other parishioners during the week.

✧ Newman's decision for a celibate life was a way of living out what he experienced as his call to holiness. Consider the challenges of integrating your sexuality with your faith. Take time to map out the decades you have lived so far. Ask yourself these questions:
✦ Have there been conversions?
✦ Has there been continuity of principles?
✦ Has this integration of sexuality and faith made sense?
✦ Has it been life-giving?

✧ While he was an Anglican, Newman's celibacy was not celebrated or affirmed by a public vow. It was something he had to choose without the supportive understanding of an ecclesial community. Take time to journal about the dimensions of your life and lifestyle that, at present, have no public stature or communal support. How do these dimensions relate to your personal call to holiness and to the whole church's call to holiness. Talk with Christ about this matter.

✧ At a time when clergy did not dress very differently from others and were addressed as "Mister," Newman believed and taught that real public witness consisted in changing society. How has your desire for God influenced your positions on public policy? Are you being called to be more actively involved in letter writing, assembling a small group, performing publicly the works of mercy, becoming a candidate for election? Discuss your reflections with a friend or with Christ, or both.

✧ What are the urgent issues or daily duties in which you are involved and in which peacefulness needs to be foregone? Invite yourself to take an hour to listen to a piece of music, paint a picture, sculpt with clay, or engage in vigorous exercise. In whatever activity you choose, let it represent the struggle. Surround this time with a petition to God for what you most need.

✧ Take your Bible and read chapter 19 of Leviticus. Notice how keeping the commandments and social relations are related to the holiness of God, and the becoming holy of God's people. Translate three verses into language that is contemporary and addresses patterns of current behavior. Share what you have done with a friend or family member.

God's Word

[God] spoke to Moses, saying:

> "Speak to all the congregation of the people of Israel and say to them: You shall be holy, for I . . . your God am holy. You shall each revere your mother and father, and you shall keep my sabbaths: I am . . . your God. Do not turn to idols or make cast images for yourselves. I am . . . your God." (Leviticus 19:1–4)

Closing prayer: Oh holy God, let me realize that my life and my world are full of your holiness. Call me to you, and call those you have given me to love, so that the whole earth is wedded to you in joy.

✧ Meditation 2 ✧

Lead, Kindly Light

Theme: Newman experienced an inner light that guided him from shadows to the truth, step-by-step. He trusted that divine providence would be with him to the end.

Opening prayer: Give me enough light to see one more step, and enough trust in you, O God, to take that step.

About Newman

All his life, Newman followed a motto from Thomas Scott: "Growth—the only evidence of life." Newman would say in the essay that led him to the Catholic church that "here below to live is to change, and to be perfect is to have changed often" (*An Essay on the Development of Christian Doctrine*, p. 40). In the choice between stagnation and fruitfulness, Newman would choose the painful process of change, not for change's sake, but for the sake of growth. This kind of change was for him maturation and the giving of life.

At times, Newman was aware that new ventures were beckoning. This was so at the end of the year in 1832, when the young Newman took time to go on a Mediterranean voyage with his friends the Froudes. He wrote:

> I went to various coasts of the Mediterranean; parted with my friends at Rome; went down for the second time to

Sicily without companion, at the end of April; and got back to England by Palermo in the early part of July. The strangeness of foreign life threw me back into myself; I found pleasure in historical sites and beautiful scenes, not in men and manners. (Newman, *Apologia*, p. 29)

In the midst of onshore visits and travel sickness, movements at sea and holdovers in ports, Newman was becoming more and more convinced that he had a mission, that he had work to do in England. Toward the end of this voyage, in a boat bound for Marseilles, Newman wrote the now well-known lines of the poem "The Pillar of the Cloud."

His next step involved spearheading the Oxford Movement, a movement of reading, writing, and publishing that would lead to a change in his religious outlook. He devoured early church history and found there the embodiment of Christian life. This was the world of bishop-theologians and martyrs who were great preachers and pastors. It was the world of the desert fathers and mothers engaged in monasticism.

But with continued study and prayer, he had to grapple with the growth and the change reflected in the history of the church. Were these inherited changes corruptions of the truth of the revelation of the mystery of God, or were they organic developments? Newman realized that if the church were alive it would have to grow, and growth would mean change. He would move to the Church of Rome when he became convinced that its present condition was an authentic development of the early church that still claimed his loyalty. But because his imagination was so powerful, Newman moved slowly to make sure that there was a real grounding for the change he could see coming within his convictions and his understanding.

In the early 1840s, Newman was in a real crisis that would not be resolved until 1845. He had no theory; he realized that his sympathies were moving toward the Church of Rome. But until he had worked through the issue of development of doctrine, his reason and his feelings were not together, and he wished to be guided by reason. When the whole of Newman was ready to change, he then moved into communion with Rome.

Pause: Reflect on changes in your own life. Were they ones you chose? What were the elements of your choice?

Newman's Words

Lead, Kindly Light, amid the encircling gloom,
    Lead Thou me on!
The night is dark, and I am far from home—
    Lead Thou me on!
Keep Thou my feet; I do not ask to see
The distant scene,—one step enough for me.

I was not ever thus, nor pray'd that Thou
    Shouldst lead me on.
I loved to choose and see my path, but now
    Lead Thou me on!
I loved the garish day, and, spite of fears,
Pride ruled my will: remember not past years.

So long Thy power hath blest me, sure it still
    Will lead me on,
O'er moor and fen, o'er crag and torrent, till
    The night is gone;
And with the morn those angel faces smile
Which I have loved long since, and lost awhile.

(Tillotson, comp., *Prose and Poetry*, p. 807)

Reflections

The poem that Newman wrote on his way home to face challenges that would change his life forever is an invocation of faith and hope. Like Newman, we may be called to embrace the dark and dramatic in our life or to admit that we are not sure where we are going. This poem may be a reflection of faith facing daily uncertainties, or a deeper prayer of surrender at those moments when we cannot see where we are going and need to trust. In this century, this poem served as an inspiration to Martin Luther King Jr. and Mahatma Gandhi who, like Newman, desired to be faithful to their conscience and to principles of justice and nonviolence in the face of expected resistance and hostility to their social action.

✧ Pray the poem "The Pillar of the Cloud" slowly and meditatively. Pause on the words or phrases that speak to you most significantly. Throughout the day, at the beginning of each hour, say softly to yourself, "Lead, Kindly Light."

✧ Reflect on those in your family, among your friends, or of your acquaintances who are discovering in themselves "a sense of mission." Write a letter to them—which you might or might not send—in the spirit that honors both reason and feelings.

✧ Look at a photo album or videos of your family. Notice how the people have changed from the way you know them now. What has lasted and grown? What has changed or disappeared? Notice the background. What is still the same? What things are different now? Journal about the changes you have noticed; finish your thoughts with a conversation with the Holy Spirit.

✧ Open the Bible to a favorite passage. How has it spoken to you over the years? Has your understanding of its meaning changed? Grown? Is there any special wisdom figure in your life connected with this passage? Thank God for the gifts that have been given through this person and passage.

✧ Examine one tradition from your past that you have kept. How does it give life today? How does it relate to your faith in God?

✧ Recall a journey or voyage you have taken in your life. Where did you go? When did you go? Who was with you? Reflect on the feelings you had when entering situations that were foreign or unfamiliar. Think about what you learned of the world, of others, or about yourself on this journey. Recall situations of specific joy and beauty, or of particular fear and discomfort. As you finish your reflections, pray to the

Holy Spirit to be with you as a kindly light to lead you on your present journey.

God's Word

Do not remember the former things,
     or consider the things of old.
I am about to do a new thing;
     now it springs forth, do you not perceive it?
(Isaiah 43:18–19)

Closing prayer: Help me, dear Creator, not to be afraid of the creative. Help me, dear Redeemer, not to be afraid of the change redemption brings. Help me, Holy Spirit, not to be afraid of the darkness and to trust such light as you give me.

✧ Meditation 3 ✧

The Venture of Faith

Theme: Newman believed that faith was more than an assent to doctrines by the mind, it was a full assent to the mysteries of God in our life. Faith was a venture that called for risk.

Opening prayer: O God of great expectations, give me such a living faith that I may freely embrace the good that I do not yet possess.

About Newman

In the 1830s, Newman preached a sermon entitled "The Ventures of Faith." In it he said the following:

> If then faith be the essence of a Christian life . . . it follows that our duty lies in risking upon Christ's word what we have, for what we have not; and doing so in a noble, generous way, not indeed rashly or lightly, still without knowing accurately what we are doing, not knowing either what we give up, nor again what we shall gain. (Newman, *Parochial and Plain Sermons*, IV, p. 299)

Newman challenged his hearers to reflect on what they had personally staked on the truth of Christ's promise.

This is the question, What have *we* ventured? I really fear, when we come to examine, it will be found that there is nothing we resolve, nothing we do, nothing we do not do, nothing we avoid, nothing we choose, nothing we give up, nothing we pursue, which we should not resolve, and do, and not do, and avoid, and choose, and give up, and pursue, if Christ had not died, and heaven were not promised us. (Newman, *Parochial and Plain Sermons*, IV, p. 301)

His own venture of faith is most publicly manifest in his move away from the Anglican church and to the Roman church. In his biography of Newman, Wilfrid Ward relates this story:

In 1843 Newman wrote to a friend definitely that he believed the Roman Catholic Church to be the Church of the Apostles. England was in schism, and such graces as were apparent in the Anglican Communion were "extraordinary and from the overflowing of the Divine dispensation" (*Apologia*, p. 208). He resigned the vicarage of St. Mary's on September 18. In the same year in the pages of the Conservative Journal he retracted all his attacks on the Church of Rome. The inevitable sequel was in sight for others as well as for himself—the parting from so many Oxford friends and disciples who had for years hung on his every word. On September 25 he preached at Littlemore his sermon on the Parting of Friends. It was the last public scene of the silent tragedy which was being enacted. He told in that sermon, clearly for those who understood, how he himself had found the Church of his birth and of his early affections wanting; how he was torn asunder between the claims of those he must leave behind and those who would follow him; that he could speak to his friends no more from that pulpit, but could only commit them to God and bid them strive to do His will. His voice broke (so the tradition runs) and his words were interrupted by the sobs of his hearers as he said his last words of farewell. (*The Life of John Henry Cardinal Newman*, I, p. 76)

Pause: Ask yourself: What have I ventured in my life of faith? Has faith influenced my present lifestyle?

Newman's Words

Our very state and warfare is one of faith. Let us aim at, let us reach after and (as it were) catch at the things of the next world. There is a voice within us, which assures us that there is something higher than earth. We cannot analyze, define, contemplate what it is that thus whispers to us. It has no shape or material form. There is that in our hearts which prompts us to religion, and which condemns and chastises sin. And this yearning of our nature is met and sustained, it finds an object to rest upon, when it hears of the existence of an All-powerful, All-gracious Creator. It incites us to a noble faith in what we cannot see. (Newman, *Parochial and Plain Sermons*, VI, pp. 339–340)

Reflection

Newman believed that human beings were by nature bound to act more on faith than on knowledge or arguments. This was simply a fact for him, and one that showed itself in most human activities. We become friends or fall in love and marry, not because of plausible arguments or extended information, but because we have faith that opens the eyes of love. We have children with no guarantees for the future, but we hope blessings will be there for them and for us. In the most humanizing of activities, faith is the primary motive for action.

Why we are like this, Newman had no idea, but he recognized that something in our heart connects us to a world higher than earth and is responsive to the existence of an ineffable Creator. He thought it natural that science and philosophy would not ground religion, but rather a message, a story, or a vision would be the foundation of our faith.

✧ Living by faith is a way to live freely. Reflect on a time of your life when you made a commitment on faith, and not because of evidence or prior experience. How did this commitment affect your inner security? How did this commitment give you the impetus to action? How did it enlighten you concerning the practical things to do? Compose a prayer of thanksgiving for the gift of faith and for the way it has been active in your life.

✧ Remember a time when you sat holding a baby or sat next to a child in his or her crib. What were your thoughts, your dreams, your concerns? What has unfolded for you and this child since that time? How does this affect your life of faith?

✧ At venturesome points of his life, Newman used phrases like, "going into the open seas" or "setting his face towards the wilderness." When, in your life, have you arrived at critical points like this? What was being ventured? What was the risk? How was God present? Spend some time with one of these memories or images, and pray for those who are at a critical moment of venturing in faith in their life now.

✧ Remember a time when you heard of the death of a beloved friend. What were your thoughts and feelings at the time? How did this event and the reality of death affect your life of faith? What questions did this raise? What graces were given at this time? How did you need to venture after it happened?

✧ "I am setting my face absolutely toward the wilderness." Imagine yourself as one of the chosen people on the edge of the desert, ready to move on a long journey toward a new and promised land. Allow yourself to repeat this phrase over and over, attending to the images and feelings that arise in your heart. Focusing on the desert, let the Spirit lead you where it will. At the end of the prayer, take a symbolic step.

✧ What or who has been an enemy to your faith? What was the struggle like? What was at stake in this battle? Sing to yourself these lines from "Amazing Grace": "Thru many dangers, toils, and snares, we have already come. 'Twas grace that brought us safe thus far, and grace will bring us home."

God's Word

Now faith is the assurance of things hoped for, the conviction of things not seen. Indeed, by faith our ancestors received approval. . . . By faith Abraham obeyed when he was called to set out for a place that he was to receive as an inheritance; and he set out, not knowing where he was going. . . . By faith he received power of procreation, even though he was too old—and Sarah herself was barren—because he considered him faithful who had promised. . . . Therefore lift your drooping hands and strengthen your weak knees, and make straight paths for your feet, so that what is lame may not be put out of joint but rather be healed. (Hebrews 11:1–2,8–11; 12:12–13)

Closing prayer:

O God, my whole life is filled with your mercies and blessings. Year after year you carry me on, remove dangers from my path, recover me, recruit me, refresh me, bear with me, direct me, sustain me, love me. (Adapted from *Meditations and Devotions of the Late Cardinal Newman*, p. 421)

✧ Meditation 4 ✧

Traveling Light in Community

Theme: For Newman, Christian faith is both a public affair and an interpersonal one. Faith is not something to be lived only in solitude, but calls us to be our true selves in community.

Opening prayer: In the beginning, Holy One, you made all things through, and for, and with your Word. Where your Word and Spirit are, there is communion. Draw me into the community that is your new creation.

About Newman

With only brief intermissions, Newman lived his long life in just three places: London, Oxford, and Birmingham. By modern standards this is not much movement because these cities are all within a few hundred miles of each other, more or less along a straight line. But in his day, they were three different worlds: one the center of the growing worldwide empire, one an ancient university town almost untouched by the industrial revolution, and the last one a city of factories and immigrants.

While at Oxford, Newman attempted to live out his life as pastor-scholar in a small college with its own chapel, and to call a community around the altar of the University Church of Saint Mary's. His life at Littlemore, the stables turned "monastery," was a transitional stage for Newman, but still a place to search for and to live in community.

Upon his reception into the Roman Catholic church, his first question was, "What community?" He did not know a lot of Catholics or much about the religious orders in Britain, but he knew the ancient church and its ideal of community life. That ancient ideal called to him.

While in Rome, Newman with his friend from Oxford days, Ambrose St. John, discovered the Oratory of Saint Philip Neri. The mission of Philip Neri was to save people not from, but in the world. In his own milieu of the sixteenth century, Philip had no desire to increase the number of religious orders, so he forbade the taking of oaths, promises, or vows. Nothing but human affection and Christian charity could bind together the community. The guidelines Philip gave were simple and practical steps for living together while serving the laity who came to the house of prayer or oratory.

With the advice of the Catholic bishop of Birmingham, Nicholas Wiseman, Newman began his life as an Oratorian in that city. He was hoping for "companions who have a good deal of fun in them," for if "we have not spirit, it will be like bottled beer with the cork out" (Ker and Gornall, eds., *Letters and Diaries*, XII, pp. 51, 54–55).

Newman recognized the Oratory of Saint Philip Neri as a place where friends could gather and the word of God become alive. The Secular Oratory, the laity who gather in response to Saint Philip's gifts, became a chief work of his own ministry. In one of the conferences with them, Newman said, "Your strength lies in your God and your conscience; therefore, it lies not in your number. . . . God saves whether by many or by few; you are to aim at showing forth His light" (John Henry Cardinal Newman, *Present Position of Catholics in England*, p. 388). These conferences with the Secular Oratory became one of Newman's best books, which he entitled *The Present Position of Catholics in England*.

So the Oratory, with its light structures, its openness to the laity, and its prayer, became a real home for Newman during the second half of his life. The cheerful Saint Philip Neri, evangelical in fervor and Catholic in culture, was a good spiritual father to the newly Romanized Newman.

Pause: To what particular local community has my faith led me? What bonds us? What are our mutual obligations?

Newman's Words

Newman gave his ideas on the centrality of community and love for one another in talks to the Oratory. He was nearly eighty years old when he said the following:

> I have never liked a large Oratory. Twelve working Priests has been the limit of my ambition. One cannot love many at one time; one cannot really have many friends. An Oratory is a family and a home; a domestic circle, as the words imply, is bounded and rounded. A family can be counted; there only, in the natural order are to be found the [familiar faces] of which our Rule speaks. A large body can hardly help breaking from its own weight. . . . We should in all Congregational matters strive to move as one mind; avoid, if possible, going by majorities; be tender of the Fathers who form a minority, while on the other hand single Fathers should not inconsiderately take advantage of the tenderness exercised towards them. Only by a tradition such as this, only by a happy gift of healing in those lacerations of heart which the law of bereavements necessarily involves, only by a moral constitution in its members thus healthy and elastic, that our Oratory will thrive. (Placid Murray, ed., *Newman the Oratorian*, p. 387)

Reflection

The idea of community was lived out in a new manner by Philip Neri as a gift of the Spirit of Christ and a sign of God's presence. At the time of Philip, others just gathered around him. Three hundred years after him, Newman chose the same simple pattern of living. It was impossible for Newman to imagine his own life as a Christian without being connected to a stable community.

The call to form community cannot be abstract for the Christian. It has to exist in some practical form in the day-to-day of life. Our struggles to love and be loved, to know and be known, are not just social; they are challenges and gifts at the heart of a Christian life of faith. Living in families, maintaining friendships, and promoting civic welfare is both humanizing and costly, as most people know.

Our culture thrives on the bonds of human affection but also creates obstacles to it. The mobility possible in our time keeps careers going, but often at the price of long-term friendships and commitments. Communications technology may be a means of maintaining human bonds, or it may be a temptation to pseudorelationships. The spirit of discernment is especially necessary in forming Christian community in our culture.

✧ Look around the place where you live. Like Newman refurbished the stables of Littlemore for a community life, are you being called to refurbish a place in your city or neighborhood as a shared space? Are you being called to remake a place in your heart for loved ones, for a family member, or for the Word of God? Are you being called to redo a room in your home as a place of study, prayer, conversation, or even dancing?

✧ The worlds in which we live are both impersonal and interpersonal. Take time to make a diagram or picture that represents the worlds you move in and through each day: home, work, stores, schools, recreational centers, church, etc. Pray about each one and reflect on the ways you relate to others in these environments. Ask the Word of God to be present in these reflections.

✧ Who is in your home circle? Should the circle be expanded? Should the circle be tightened? Reread Newman's words and relate them to your own home circle. Compose a prayer for the spirit of your family.

✧ When Newman was living away from his Birmingham community, he stayed in touch by letter, periodic visits, or written conference articles. Spend time evaluating your community relations and your methods of long-distance communication. Pray for those on your mind. Mail a card, write a letter, e-mail, visit, or phone a few people who have entered your thoughts.

✧ In our culture, parish communities are not always places where persons know each other. Are there any efforts you can make to put names with faces, to get to know and be known by a few persons there, to gather a larger group as a faith community? Make a three-month resolution that will help form, or re-form, this parish community, and share your resolution with two friends.

God's Word

I thank my God every time I remember you, constantly praying with joy in every one of my prayers for all of you. . . . It is right for me to think this way about all of you, because you hold me in your heart, for all of you share in God's grace with me. . . . For God is my witness, how I long for all of you with the compassion of Christ Jesus. And this is my prayer, that your love may overflow more and more with knowledge and full insight to help you to determine what is best, so that in the day of Christ you may be pure and blameless, having produced the harvest of righteousness that comes through Jesus Christ for the glory and praise of God. (Philippians 1:3–11)

Closing prayer: Spirit of God, you are in love, as love, for love. Let love re-create me for the sake of faithfulness to community. Let love cast out all fear and lead me to you with all my friends and family.

✧ Meditation 5 ✧

Education in Faith

Theme: Education in faith is education of both the heart and the mind. Newman highlighted the importance of both.

Opening prayer: Spirit of God, you are the spirit of truth and the spirit of love. The fire you bring is the flame of love and the light of truth. Come, Holy Spirit.

About Newman

Newman made a bold statement about his Oxford experience when he said: "Catholics did not make us Catholics; Oxford made us Catholics" (Charles S. Dessain, ed., *Letters and Diaries of John Henry Newman*, XIX, p. 352). Oxford did this by simply being a good place to get an education.

In his early years, Newman personally knew his instructors, remembering later in his life their names and their influence on him. They taught him not so much what to think as how to think. In his twenties at Oxford, Newman enjoyed a learning community. Oxford provided an environment in which, together with others, he could study, write, discuss, and carry out his tutoring responsibilities.

In the academic year 1828–1829, Newman got himself in trouble with the Oriel provost, Hawkins, as he revamped the tutorial system with his fellows. Newman took the initiative to create and implement a system that, first of all, matched a limited number of students with a tutor who would provide lectures, tutoring, and mentoring specifically to these few. Second, the tutors would work with one another, opening up their own lectures to the students matched with another tutor. It was a personalized system that Newman judged a better accommodation to the real needs of young students. It was an arrangement that demanded close collaboration of the tutors.

The provost did not agree with the principles involved; he wanted lectures open to all students indiscriminately, and tutoring to focus primarily on intellectual skills and mastering the curriculum. To deal with this situation, the provost just stopped assigning students to Newman.

Cut off from tutoring students, Newman set up informal lectures in the chapel of the university church. Along with these, as a curate, he provided Sunday evensong services that became popular because of his preaching. In the pulpit he was not dramatic or flamboyant. He was very steady and quiet in his presentation. But students hung on his words because they knew he meant them, tried to live them, and had God at the center of the enterprise.

Later, as a Catholic priest, while having some difficulties with the Irish bishops over the founding of their university in Dublin, Newman again took to lectures. Some of the same ideas about education were still as vibrant in him as they had been in his Oxford days:

> If I had to choose between a so-called University, which dispensed with residence and tutorial superintendence, and gave its degrees to any person who passed an examination in a wide range of subjects, and a University which had no professors or examinations at all, but merely brought a number of young . . . together for three or four years, and then sent them away. . . . If I were asked which of these two methods was the better discipline of the intellect, . . . if I must determine which of the two courses was the more successful in training, moulding, enlarging the mind, . . . I have no hesitation in giving the preference to that University which did nothing, over that which exacted of its members an acquaintance with

every science under the sun. (John Henry Cardinal Newman, *The Idea of a University*, p. 145)

His whole life long, Newman had a great intellectual curiosity combined with a great capacity for friendship. He learned the deepest principles of scholarship and religion not in the content of tutorials or exams, but in the people he met, came to respect, and even love in that educational environment. For Newman, a university is primarily a community of loving wisdom.

Pause: Does education mean schooling to you or does it mean formation within a learning community?

Newman's Words

No book can convey the special spirit and delicate peculiarities of its subject with that rapidity and certainty which attend on the sympathy of mind with mind, through the eyes, the look, the accent, and the manner, in casual expressions thrown off at the moment, and the unstudied turns of familiar conversation. . . . The general principles of any study you may learn by books at home; but the detail, the colour, the tone, the air, the life which makes it live in us, you must catch all these from those in whom it lives already. (John Henry Cardinal Newman, *Historical Sketches*, III, pp. 8–9)

Reflections

Newman gives us a chance to consider a life of faith in relation to education. Within the Christian heritage, we understand that the word of God became incarnate in Jesus of Nazareth. The Christian Testament portrait of Jesus shows him teaching his followers like a Jewish rabbi instructing and living with his disciples. We can expect that significant teachers embody in themselves the lessons they teach us. A good preacher or teacher attempts to bring home to the listeners the message they have already brought home to themselves.

Like many institutions at the close of the second millennium, education is in great flux or even crisis. Newman is a reminder that the principles guiding policies need to be brought to light, and that faith is not opposed to the mind and heart's search for truth. The best education will be given in a community where values and faith are not just taught but caught. His ideas on education are important both in school and nonschool settings. Sunday worship assemblies, catechetical centers, family life, and civic events are forums where formation and education overlap.

✧ Newman said, "Catholics did not make us Catholic. Oxford made us Catholic." What in your life has made you Catholic? What continues to make you Catholic?

✧ Take time to list ten things you like to do. Review the list, noting if you learned the activities in school or out of school. Review the list again, asking yourself, "Who was my teacher?" Close with a prayer of thanksgiving for these activities that you enjoy.

✧ Call to mind the best teacher you ever had. Reflect on what he or she embodied for you, and how he or she related to you. In the days and weeks ahead, take time to write and illustrate a child's book about this teacher. Share it with a younger person you know.

✧ Have you ever been involved in a situation where people's minds spontaneously played off of each other while exploring a topic or implementing a project? How did you and the group feel at the end of the session? Reread Newman's words on his preferred mode of education. Pray for those involved in education today.

✧ Read Matthew 7:24–29 in the following "God's Word" section. See and hear Jesus "speaking with authority." Imagine the two houses: one built on rock, the other built on sand. Imagine the storm coming up. Imagine the outcome. What lesson does this parable hold for you about education and faith?

God's Word

"Everyone then who hears these words of mine and acts on them will be like a wise [person] who built [a] house on rock. The rain fell, the floods came, and the winds blew and beat on that house, but it did not fall, because it had been founded on rock. And everyone who hears these words of mine and does not act on them will be like a foolish [person] who built [a] house on sand. The rain fell, and the floods came, and the winds blew and beat against that house, and it fell—and great was its fall!" Now when Jesus had finished saying these things, the crowds were astounded at his teaching, for he taught them as one having authority. (Matthew 7:24–29)

Closing prayer:

Loving Wisdom, lead me from strength to strength, gently, sweetly, tenderly, lovingly, powerfully, effectually, until you finally bring me to yourself. (Adapted from *Meditations and Devotions,* p. 398)

Becoming Like God

Theme: For Newman, grace was the life of God transforming humans into divine likeness; grace was not only a notion in his mind, but a reality in his life.

Opening prayer: God of life and growth, we grow into your likeness as your grace transforms us by your holy presence that is beyond our imagination. Help us to glimpse even a small part of what you are doing within us.

About Newman

Newman's life as an Anglican was transformed by his discovery of the early church. Whately, fellow at Oriel and later archbishop of Dublin, taught Newman that the church was a substantive body, independent of the state or nation. Keble taught him that faith and love are directed toward an object and in the vision of that object they live. Froude directed his attention to tradition as an instrument of religious teaching.

With these thoughts in Newman's mind, a new project appeared in 1830. Hugh Rose, a noted Anglican preacher at Cambridge, made a proposal to him to write a book on the history of the principal church councils as part of a series for a theological library. Newman accepted the project and began his work on the Council of Nicaea. In preparation he read the

Fathers of the Church, jotted down citations, and composed his work. This study became the book *Arians of the Fourth Century*, published in 1832.

What specifically attracted Newman at this time was the Church of Alexandria and the works of the early Greek theologians Origen, Clement, and Athanasius.

> Some portions of their teaching, magnificent in themselves, came like music to my inward ear, as if the response to ideas, which, with little external to encourage them, I had cherished so long. These were based on the mystical or sacramental principle, and spoke of the various Economies or Dispensations of the Eternal. I understood these passages to mean that the exterior world, physical and historical, was but the manifestation to our senses of realities greater than itself. (Newman, *Apologia*, p. 24)

Newman's discovery of the early church did not lead him to ignore his experience, but enabled him to speak about it and explore its depths. The writings, especially of Athanasius, gave him the realization that the connection between Christ and Christians is so intimate that the language that belongs to the Incarnate Word really belongs to them. He also began to understand that in the early church, the pressure of controversy elicited and developed a truth which was held by Christians, but it was not perfectly realized and not yet publicly acknowledged.

Newman's understanding of grace as God's presence transforming humanity affected the message of his preaching. When he spoke on "Sincerity and Hypocrisy," he reminded his listeners,

> A true Christian, or one who is in a state of acceptance with God, is he, who, in such sense, has faith in [God], as to live in the thought that [God] is present with him,— present not externally, not in nature merely, or in providence, but in his innermost heart. (Newman, *Parochial and Plain Sermons*, V, p. 226)

Pause: How am I aware of God's presence in me? Have I ever had the experience of something exterior to myself coming as music to my innermost heart?

Newman's Words

We are members of another world . . . brought into that invisible kingdom of Christ which faith alone discerns,—that mysterious Presence of God which encompasses us, which is in us, and around us, which is in our heart, which enfolds us as though with a robe of light, hiding our scarred and discoloured souls from the sight of Divine Purity, and making them shining as the Angels; and which flows in upon us too by means of all forms of beauty and grace which this visible world contains, in a starry host or (if I may so say) a milky way of divine companions, the inhabitants of Mount Zion, where we dwell. (Newman, *Parochial and Plain Sermons,* IV, pp. 228–229)

This presence of God is the grounding of an inner peace:

The foundations of the ocean, the vast realms of water which girdle the earth, are as tranquil and as silent in the storm as in a calm. So it is with the souls of [the] holy. They have a well of peace springing up within them unfathomable; and though the accidents of the hour may make them seem agitated, yet in their hearts they are not so. (Newman, *Parochial and Plain Sermons,* V, p. 69)

Reflection

In reading the Fathers of the Church, Newman found an excitement, an awakening, and a confirmation of the faith that already lived in his heart. It was like the presence of a lover to the beloved, the beloved to the lover. In this type of presence, many things, even something as simple as a letter, can carry great emotional significance and transformational power. Fortunately for us, Newman not only knew this transforming presence of God, he was able to speak of it in his writings and sermons.

In his activity, Newman gives us a model of reform, not unlike that given by other reformers. Renewal often comes by the exploration of our roots, the return to the sources, the retraveling in imagination and thought of the paths taken in the early church. This move is a recovery of a living tradition, and entry through the words into the mysteries of the Trinity, the Incarnation, and the sacramental principle. Newman has showed us that conservation of the truths of faith implies continued growth and fruition, and that church reform is essentially and wonderfully conservative.

✧ Reflect on the meaning of the ancient mass prayer: "By the mystery of this water and wine may we come to share in the divinity of Christ, who humbled himself to share in our humanity." Repeat this phrase over and over as a prayer of the heart.

✧ Go to a library or bookstore and find a theological book, preferably one of the writings of the early church fathers. Spend an extended time reading, noticing how you are or are not moved by what you read. Spend some time reviewing this experience in your mind and heart.

✧ Read the following "God's Word" section. Reflect on Christ's real presence. Be silent and reverent in this prayer.

✧ Candles are lit in front of icons, as well as in front of the reserved Eucharist. Light a candle in honor of God's presence within you. Meditate on the light within and without. If you are moved to do so, sing a very quiet version of "This Little Light of Mine."

✧ Preachers like to use the comparison of window glass to speak of God's light present to us and to others. Some windows are smudgy and block the light, others are clear and transparent. Take time to wash a window, thanking God for the gift of light and asking for removal of your "smudges."

✧ The God that Newman loved and served was the creator of the universe. Place yourself in a location where you can appreciate the beauties of nature, and pray spontaneously or pray Psalm 8.

God's Word

Do you not know that you are God's temple and that God's Spirit dwells in you? . . . For God's temple is holy, and you are that temple. (1 Corinthians 3:16–17)

Closing prayer:

Praise to the Holiest in the height,
And in the depths be praise.
All God's words are wonderful;
Most sure are all God's ways.
(Adapted from "The Dream of Gerontius" in Tillotson, comp., *Prose and Poetry*, p. 831)

✧ Meditation 7 ✧

What Am I Living For?

Theme: Depression and doubts about his place in the church dogged Newman almost his entire life as a Catholic. His intellectual appreciation of his faith and the church did not prevent his suffering, but within the suffering he continued to trust in God.

Opening prayer: Compassionate God, when we sense there is nothing at all for us, hold on to us.

About Newman

Although Newman most appreciated tranquil and amiable community life, his years as an Oratorian were all but that. In 1856, he was in Dublin, and after three weeks still had not unpacked his belongings. He says:

> My letters are a daily burden, and, did I not answer them by return of post, they would soon get my head under water and drown me. Every hour or half hour of the day I have people calling on me. I have to entertain strangers at dinner, I have to attend inaugural Lectures. . . . I have to stop Professors resigning, and Houses revolting. I have to keep accounts and find money, when I have none. . . . I have to lecture on Latin Composition, and examine for Exhibitions. In ten days I rush to Birmingham for their

sheer want of me—and then have to throw myself into quite a fresh world. And I have the continual pain of our Fathers sighing if I am not there, and priests and professors looking blank if I am not here. (Ker and Gornall, eds., *Letters and Diaries*, XVII, pp. 447–448)

The thirty-year span of Newman's most active time as a Catholic corresponded with the last half of his life. During these decades, he experienced the diminishments of aging, losses from death and changed circumstances, and the frequent turnaround of major projects instigated by other church officials and then dropped.

The situations were public: the Achilli trial that could have sent him to prison for libel, the offer mentioned and then never mentioned again of Episcopal ordination, the Bible translation project, the rectorship of the Catholic University in Dublin, the refusal to allow him back in to Oxford to found an oratory, and so on. But his reactions were mostly private. He suffered bouts of depression and terrible spiritual dryness resulting from feelings of isolation—feelings founded in fact.

In 1861, Newman reflected on all his failures. He realized his jaw had become hardened, giving him a look of sternness. He was ill, and in response to that he went to the doctor, he took a vacation, he even papered his room and put in double windows to keep out the chill. Yet as he awoke one morning and lay in bed, he asked himself: "What is the good of all this? What is to come of it? What am I living for? What am I doing for any religious end?" (Henry Tristram, ed., *John Henry Newman: Autobiographical Writings*, p. 254). He had hit bottom; everything had come to naught.

As years passed and other daily activities engaged him, his feelings mellowed and his expectations lessened. In his journal of 1874, when age was making him weaker and less capable, he acknowledged that he was probably *passé.* Yet at this time of his life, he says the psalm that most suited him was the one of the young child on his mother's lap, content and peaceful.

Pause: Am I, too, overworked and overwhelmed in carrying out my responsibilities? What are my sufferings? Where do I find peace?

Newman's Words

God has created me to do Him some definite service; He has committed some work to me which He has not committed to another. I have my mission—I never may know it in this life, but I shall be told it in the next. Somehow I am necessary for His purposes, as necessary in my place as an Archangel in his—if, indeed, I fail, He can raise another, as He could make the stones children of Abraham. Yet I have a part in this great work; I am a link in a chain, a bond of connexion between persons. He has not created me for naught. I shall do good, I shall do His work; I shall be an angel of peace, a preacher of truth in my own place, while not intending it, if I do but keep His commandments and serve Him in my calling.

Therefore, I will trust Him. Whatever, wherever I am, I can never be thrown away. If I am in sickness, my sickness may serve Him; in perplexity, my perplexity may serve Him; if I am in sorrow, my sorrow may serve Him. My sickness, or perplexity, or sorrow may be necessary causes of some great end, which is quite beyond us. He does nothing in vain; He may prolong my life, He may shorten it; He knows what He is about. He may take away my friends, He may throw me among strangers, He may make me feel desolate, make my spirits sink, hide the future from me—still He knows what He is about. (*Meditations and Devotions*, pp. 301–302)

Reflection

Newman was known for his good cheer during the crises of the Catholic university days, and his serenity at other times, but it was at a cost. Because of his great gifts, what he did produce for the church seems monumental to us living more than a century later. But he alone knew then what he could do and could not do; he noticed how his work was received and not received; he understood the cost to his conscience if he did or did not do it. Besides the writing and the pastoral care he gave, his faithfulness is another great memorial.

The kind of personality that we have been given will remain a profound mystery in Providence. Some personalities are more suitable to hard times than others. But we are all called to faithfulness despite the presence of real crosses in our life. What God can do with the crosses we bear we often do not get to see. Just knowing that Newman and others had their time of trial in union with Jesus puts us in a holy place when we are burdened.

✧ Invite Newman into your prayer and speak to him about your place in the church and your feelings and thoughts about it. Share your struggles and joys. Listen to his experience as you prayerfully dialog. If it is helpful, write out your imaginary conversation with him as a one-act play.

✧ Recall someone you have known whose sufferings were part of their hope and reliance on God. How did they love in the midst of those times? How has their example affected you? Collect stories of hope for your journal or for a small book.

✧ What psalms, songs, or poems mean the most to you in times of suffering? Pray some of them today, mindful of your own pain or the pain of others. Each evening for a week, remember others who are suffering and join your suffering to theirs.

✧ On Good Friday, when the cross is venerated, you approach it in a gesture of honor. What do you bring to Christ on the Cross? Look at the Good Friday ritual and prayers; the intercessions may be used any time and place. Pray them today, and compose some intercessions of your own.

✧ What organizations do you belong to that help alleviate suffering or the conditions that promote it? Take some time to pray for those in the organization and to write them a note of encouragement and thanks. Perhaps you could invite workers in these organizations to come and speak to your Bible study or prayer group.

God's Word

Yahweh, my heart has no false pride;
my eyes do not look too high.
I am not concerned with great affairs
or things far above me.
It is enough for me to keep my soul still and quiet
like a child in its mother's arms,
as content as a child that has been weaned.
Israel, hope in Yaweh,
now and for always!

(Psalm 131)

Closing prayer:

Emmanuel, Holy Wisdom, I give myself to you. I trust
you completely. I am born to serve you, to be yours, and
to fulfill a mission. I ask not to know what that purpose is,
I simply ask you to use me for it. (Adapted from *Meditations and Devotions*, p. 302)

Conscience

Theme: If Newman's life had only one theme, conscience would probably be it. His explanation and defense of conscience is a great gift to us. Conscience is the messenger from God, who, both in nature and grace, speaks to us from within us.

Opening prayer: God of light and peace, you are at the center of our life and never leave us alone to act in darkness and disturbance. Help us to respond to the gift you make of yourself in the center of our ongoing life.

About Newman

Newman was aware of his own conscience as a principle within him. In 1844, while still an Anglican, he wrote to his friend Edward Pusey:

"I have had a conviction, weaker or stronger, but on the whole constantly growing, and at present very strong, that we [Anglicans] are not part of the Catholic Church. I am too much accustomed to this idea to feel pain at it. I could only feel pain, if I found it led me to action. At present I do not feel any such call. Such feelings are not hastily to be called convictions, though this seems to me to be such. Did I ever arrive at a full persuasion that it was such, then I should be anxious and much perplexed." (Ian Ker, *John Henry Newman: A Biography,* p. 284)

The most dramatic choice to follow his conscience despite all costs was, of course, his abandonment of the Church of England and his reception into a not very friendly Catholic church in 1845.

As the years went on, the divine authority present to him in conscience was correlated with the divine authority present in the visible church. A critical point came in 1870, when papal infallibility was defined by the first Vatican Council. The council had been called in the middle of the military and political campaign that would unite Italy as one nation. The Papal States had been a politically independent territory, governed by the pope as a secular head of state. This territory was forcibly taken from Pius IX when he resisted the revolution. The first Vatican Council was never finished because it was interrupted by Italian troops entering Rome and finishing off the Papal States as a large politically independent territory. The pope was left with the small territory of Vatican City.

The result of this interruption was a one-sided council that defined papal authority without ever saying much about the role of bishops and the rest of the church. It could have been a disaster for the Catholic church except that moderates such as Newman prevailed in interpreting the definition and in counseling patience until another council could finish the work of defining the role of the bishops and the Christian faithful, the laity.

Newman had been opposed to the definition of papal infallibility because of the trouble it would create in its interpretation. Councils generally defined matters that were in controversy. The controversy in the nineteenth century was about the pope's secular power. But once the definition was forthcoming, Newman accepted it and helped to elucidate it.

In the political world of England, the chief opposition came from William Gladstone, the prime minister. He wrote that the political consequences of papal infallibility meant that Catholics would have to do anything the pope commanded and therefore could not be faithful to the laws of their own countries. For Newman, Gladstone's position meant that he had to exercise his own conscience and answer Gladstone. Newman knew that this would potentially offend those Catholic extremists who wanted papal infallibility to be the answer to political choices and the replacement of personal conscience.

In a public letter to the Duke of Norfolk, the senior Peer of the House of Lords and a Catholic, Newman gave a profound interpretation of church office as correlated with conscience. He speaks of that

> most serious doctrine, the right and the duty of following that Divine Authority, the voice of conscience, on which in truth the Church [itself] is built. . . . Did the pope speak against conscience in the true sense of the word, he would commit a suicidal act. He would be cutting the ground from under his feet. His very mission is to proclaim the moral law, and to protect and strengthen that "Light which enlighteneth every man that cometh into the world." On the law of conscience and its sacredness are founded both his authority in theory and his power in fact. (Newman, *Difficulties Felt by Anglicans*, II, p. 252)

In answering Gladstone's specific issue, Newman writes: "But a Pope is not infallible in his laws, nor in his commands, nor in his acts of state, nor in his administration, nor in his public policy. Let it be observed that the Vatican Council has left him just as it found him here" (Newman, *Difficulties Felt by Anglicans*, II, p. 256).

Newman's conclusion to the section on conscience in his public letter to the Duke of Norfolk was clear and concise: "I add one remark. Certainly, if I am obliged to bring religion into after-dinner toasts, (which indeed does not seem quite the thing) I shall drink—to the Pope, if you please,—still, to Conscience first, and to the Pope afterwards" (Newman, *Difficulties Felt by Anglicans*, II, p. 261).

Pause: Ask yourself, Do I think of conscience as the messenger of God, planted in the intelligence of all reasonable creatures?

Newman's Words

Conscience is not a long-sighted selfishness, nor a desire to be consistent with oneself; but it is a messenger from Him, who, both in nature and in grace, speaks to us behind a veil, and teaches and rules us by His representatives. Conscience is the aboriginal Vicar of Christ, a prophet in its informations, a monarch in its peremptoriness, a priest in its blessings and anathemas, and, even though the eternal priesthood throughout the Church could cease to be, in it the sacerdotal principle would remain and would have a sway. (Newman, *Difficulties Felt by Anglicans*, II, pp. 248–249)

Reflections

Newman realized that conscience had its counterfeits. Utility, expedience, the happiness of the greatest number, state convenience, fitness, order, the beautiful: none of these are the rule and measure of duty. Rather, there is a principle in our nature that speaks and judges, a voice to be heard, a messenger to be attended to. Newman himself said that conscience was too profound for literature and too subtle for science.

In a country where individualism rules and isolates us from one another, it is easy to think of conscience as determined by personal choice and taste. Newman took a contrary position. For Newman, conscience is the voice of the Creator within us, a principle capable of growth and refinement, a vector toward truth and goodness in our actions, and a source of inner peace. Conscience, in Newman's sense, can be a solace and support for anyone struggling to live with integrity.

✧ Reflect on the lives of three people you know who have lived out the demands of conscience when society has been most against them. What was their inspiration? What kept them going? How did they pray? What parts of the Scriptures were significant to them? What good did they do? Perhaps make a scrapbook or a collage about the life of one of them and share it with a group you belong to or a younger member of your family.

✧ Look into the poetry and spiritual songs of the downtrodden. How do they project resistance to evil while avoiding greater violence?

✧ What authority do you accept in your life? How is it life-giving? How do you know? Write your reflections to these questions in your journal.

✧ How do you experience the social pressures against conscience? When have you violated your own conscience? How did you reconcile? What did you learn? Talk with Christ about this matter.

✧ Choose a scriptural passage that speaks to you about God's right prevailing. Write it out or illustrate it in some form. How can you promote this value of your faith?

God's Word

Now who will harm you if you are eager to do what is good? But even if you do suffer for doing what is right, you are blessed. Do not fear what they fear, and do not be intimidated, but in your hearts sanctify Christ. . . . Always be ready to make your defense to anyone who demands from you an accounting for the hope that is in you; yet do it with gentleness and reverence. Keep your conscience clear, so that, when you are maligned, those who abuse you for your good conduct in Christ may be put to shame. For it is better to suffer for doing good, if suffering should be God's will, than to suffer for doing evil. (1 Peter 3:13–17)

Closing prayer: Let me hear your voice, God, in the hope that is within me. Give me gentleness, reverence, and strength to defend that hope. Amen.

Child of Joy

Theme: The capacity for joy is a gift of the Holy Spirit. Newman possessed that capacity for joy that children were especially able to bring out in him.

Opening prayer: Loving God, your Word came to us as a child while angels sang to astonished shepherds. Help us to rejoice in you and to hear the singing of angels. Overcome our doubts and hesitations.

About Newman

When Newman was just a child, he enjoyed drawing cartoon-like characters. His inventiveness, wit, and spirit of fun came out at times in his letters. When he was a boy of fourteen, Newman wrote to his sister Harriet:

Tell Jemima
Once upon a time a
Letter came from her pen
And I did not answer it then:

Therefore tell her I'm her debtor
Of a long agreeable letter.
Of pleasant school and different places
I'll inform her how the case is:

Please do send me then a letter, a
Nice epistle: Yours et cetera
      John H. Newman

(Ward, *Young Mr. Newman,* pp. 9–10)

The humor and rhythm seem to mark not only the spirit of Newman's childhood, but his spontaneous spirit whenever he was with those with whom he felt a familiarity.

In Newman's Anglican days, visitors to Oxford were happy to come into the house of the famous professor Edward Pusey and to hear that the rising star of the university, John Henry Newman, was there too. But if they had wanted to engage him in serious conversation, they were disappointed. While they talked at the parlor table with Pusey, Newman went and sat in an easy chair so he could bounce the two Pusey children on his knees and let them play with his glasses. It was a shock for the visitors, but typical of Newman who detested "humbug" and did not want the children's time with him ruined.

Newman's first pastoral experience was as a deacon and young curate at Saint Clement's. His concern for the parishioners was shown by his routine of home visitation; his concern for the children was manifested in his desire that they attend services. The church gallery was renovated for their use, and Newman assembled ninety-five of them: a dedicated act for one whose main assignment in church was to preach!

When Newman moved to the Littlemore parish outside of Oxford, he took upon himself the religious education of the children.

He wrote to a friend on 10 March 1840, "I despair almost. The top girls hardly know Adam from Noah." And to his sister Jemima on 12 March, he wrote, "I have been reforming, or at least lecturing against uncombed hair, and dirty faces and hands; but I find I am not deep in the philosophy of school-girl tidiness," and on the next day: "Can you suggest any method of bringing children [to be] punctual, besides going to their parents and making a talk? . . . How far is it good to apply [a] system of bribing? . . . Can you give me any hints in this matter?" (Ward, *Young Mr. Newman,* pp. 362–363).

By 1 April 1840, some improvements are starting to show:

> The children are improving in their singing. I have had
> the audacity to lead them and teach them some new
> tunes. Also I have rummaged out a violin and strung it
> . . . begun to *lead* them with it, a party of between twen-
> ty and thirty, great and little. . . . I have just begun
> chanting . . . Gregorian chant which the children seem
> to take to. (Ward, *Young Mr. Newman,* p. 363)

The singing seemed to impress all who attended the services at Littlemore. A warmhearted parish community sprang
up around Newman because of his work and presence there.
In his last sermon, Newman recalls: "It was a glad time when
we first met here,—many of us now present recollect it; nor
did our rejoicing cease, but was renewed every autumn, as the
day came round. . . . We have kept the feast heretofore with
merry hearts" (Ward, *Young Mr. Newman,* p. 401). Newman
then continued the sermon, recalling the words of the Exodus,
preparing for a new phase of journey.

Pause: Where do I find joy in my life? Who are the people
who evoke it?

Newman's Words

The letters that Newman wrote to children reflect the joyful-
ness that was within him, and that they in particular evoked.
He wrote in 1859 to Eleanor Bretherton, a young lady who
was "abbess for the day," celebrating Holy Innocents Day at
her convent school:

> My dear Lady Abbess,
>   I wish your Venerableness as many returns of the du-
> ties and honors of this day as is good for your said V's
> soul and body, for honors sometimes turn the head, and
> duties sometimes distract the brain.
>   Also I hope you have grown well into your monastic
> habit, and that it fits you, and that you move easy in it.
>   I hope too you can give a good account of 2 young
> nuns or novices, who belong to your community, and

who, I have reason to hope, do not give you much trouble, but on the contrary by their gravity and exactness are a consolation to your Venerableness. Especially take care that they are very tidy. And, in consequence of the great austerity of life which you commonly practise, allow yourself in some indulgence in this festive season, and do not scruple to eat a small piece of Christmas pudding, or other good things which come in your way—for Christmas comes but once a year—

Accept the assurance of my distinguished consideration.

Yours most politely, John H. Newman
(Joyce Sugg, ed., *A Packet of Letters*, pp. 116–117)

When Newman received a copy of Lewis Carroll's *Hunting of the Snark* from Helen Church, whose father was an old friend of Newman's and now dean of Saint Paul's, London, he sent this letter:

My dear Helen,
Let me thank you and your Sisters without delay, for the amusing specimen of imaginative nonsense which came to me from you and them this morning. Also, as being your gift, it shows that you have not forgotten me, though a considerable portion of your lives has past since you saw me. And, in thanking you, I send you also my warmest Easter greetings and good wishes.

The little book is not all of it nonsense; it has two pleasant prefixes of another sort. One of them is the "Inscription to a dear child"; the style of which, in words and manner, is so entirely of the School of Keble, that it could not have been written had the Christian Year [poems by Keble] never made its appearance.

The other, "the Easter greeting to every child etc.," is likely to touch the hearts of old men more than of those for whom it is intended. I recollect well my own thoughts and feelings, such as the author describes, as I lay in my crib in the early spring, with outdoor scents, sounds and sights wakening me up, and especially the cheerful ring of the mower's scythe on the lawn, which Milton long before me had noted;—and how in coming down stairs slowly, for I brought down both feet on each step, I said to myself "This is June!" though what my particular experience of June was, and how it was broad enough to be a matter of reflection, I really cannot tell.

Can't you, Mary, and Edith recollect something of the same kind? though you may not think so much of it as I do now?

May the day come for all of us, of which Easter is the promise, when that first spring may return to us, and a sweetness which cannot die may gladden our garden.

Ever Yrs affectionately John H. Newman
(Sugg, ed., *A Packet of Letters*, pp. 199–200)

And last is a ditty he wrote to another young lady, Charlotte Bowden, upon the receipt of a cake she sent to the Oratory on Saint Philip Neri's feast day:

Who is it that moulds and makes
Round, and crisp, and fragrant cakes?
Makes them with a kind intent,
As a welcome compliment,
And the best that she can send
To a venerable friend
One it is, for whom I pray,
On St. Philip's festal day,
With a loving heart that she
Perfect as her cakes may be,
Full and faithful in the round
Of her duties ever found
Where a trial comes, between
Truth and falsehood cutting keen;
Yet that keenness and completeness
Tempering with a winning sweetness.
Here's a rhyming letter, Chat,
Gift for a gift, and tit for tat.

JHN
(Sugg, ed., *A Packet of Letters*, p. 141)

Reflection

In spiritual direction and on retreats, generally a time is set aside to recollect an experience of wholeness and joy that happened to

us when we were children. Having recollected such an experience, we thank God and then ask ourselves if we really trust it as
something upon which to build our life. Throughout Newman's
long life, he could reach out to children with great gentleness
and recollect his own imaginative and deeply felt childhood.

In the Scriptures, the disciples of Jesus are ready to send
the children away. Jesus responds by calling the children to
himself, and remarking that "it is to such as these that the
kingdom of heaven belongs" (Matthew 19:14). Sometimes we
can push our childhood experiences aside when they would
otherwise be sources of blessing and trust. Even the English
author Charles Dickens, in *A Christmas Carol,* has the ghost of
Christmas past take Scrooge back to a time when the old miser
was younger and kinder.

Children have a remarkable resilience, a toughness that
comes from being in touch with their inner self, despite their
own fears and dependency. They are able to be joyful because
everything in them says that we are made for joy and that the
bad times are intrusions, no matter how ferocious.

✧ Set aside a definite time to be with children, your own
or others'. Make it a joyful, playful event that invites spon-
taneity. Before the end of the day, recall the surprises the children brought to you, the surprises you brought to yourself.

✧ Write a comic, rhyming poem to celebrate some holi-
day or anniversary. Get a rhyming dictionary, if necessary, to
help you. Explore the fun that comes with this addition to the
party. Philip Neri, the founder of Newman's Oratorian community, used to have stories read, songs sung, and jigs danced
for visitors when he thought things were getting too serious.

✧ Every day write down three things that made you
happy that day. At the end of a week, you will have twenty-
one items. At the end of the year, you will have a list of more
than a thousand things. Pray over this list. Eucharist means
thanksgiving. Bring the list to your Eucharist.

✧ Keep a file folder of the things made by children for
you. Plan to give them back a decade or two later.

God's Word

The wolf shall live with the lamb,
    the leopard shall lie down with the kid,
    the calf and thc lion and the fatling together,
    and a little child shall lead them.
The cow and the bear shall graze,
    their young shall lie down together;
    and the lion shall eat straw like the ox.
The nursing child shall play over the hole of the asp,
    and the weaned child shall put its hand on the
        adder's den.
They will not hurt or destroy
    on all my holy mountain;
for the earth will be full of the knowledge of the LORD
    as the waters cover the sea.

(Isaiah 11:6–9)

Closing prayer:

O my God and Savior, in your arms I am safe. Give me up and I have nothing to hope for. Keep me and I have nothing to fear. (Adapted from *Meditations and Devotions*, p. 199)

The Word of God

Theme: Newman's faith was nourished by the word of God. He was a preacher who could make the scriptural word come alive for his hearers. We turn to the Scriptures not only to have the words come alive for us, but to have the Word bring us life.

Opening prayer: Speak to us, O Word of God. Your servants are listening.

About Newman

Along with his own personal engagement with the narratives of the Scriptures and his extensive study of the doctrine of the word of God in the early church, Newman spent most of his life preaching the word of God. He considered it a serious and sacred duty, and appeared publicly to be both serene and eloquent in his sermons.

A friend and acquaintance of Newman wrote of him in 1881:

> I had then never seen so impressive a person. I met him now and then in private; I attended his church and heard him preach Sunday after Sunday; he is supposed to have been insidious, to have led his disciples on to conclusions

to which he designed to bring them, while his purpose was carefully veiled. He was, on the contrary, the most transparent of men. He told us what he believed to be true. He did not know where it would carry him. (Anne Mozley, ed., *Letters and Correspondence of John Henry Newman*, II, p. 442)

Newman believed in the importance of personal engagement with the word of God, not only at times of liturgy but in the movements of grace in prayer. He counseled a young woman who was seeking his advice:

Nothing is more painful than that sense of unreality which you describe. I believe one especial remedy for it is to give a certain time of the day to meditation, though the cure is, of course, very uncertain. However, you should not attempt it without a good deal of consideration and a fair prospect of going on steadily with it. What I mean is the giving half an hour every morning to the steady contemplation of some *one* sacred subject. . . . You should begin by strongly impressing on your mind that you are in Christ's Presence. . . . Of course, there is the greatest care necessary to do all this with extreme reverence, not as an experiment, or a kind of prescription or charm.

(Mozley, ed., *Letters and Correspondence*, II, p. 383)

Newman realized that culture has had a great influence both on thoughts and on imagination. But engagement with the word of God can remold our thoughts and our imagination as well as move us to action.

By obeying the commands of Scripture, we learn that these commands really come from God; by trying we make proof; by doing we come to know. . . . Those who try to obey God evidently gain a knowledge of themselves at least; and this may be shown to be the first and principal step towards knowing God. (Newman, *Parochial and Plain Sermons*, VIII, pp. 112–113, 116)

Pause: How does the Word of God come to me? How well do I listen?

Newman's Words

We get acquainted with some one whom God employs to bring before us a number of truths which were closed on us before; and we but half understand them, and but half approve of them; and yet God seems to speak in them, and Scripture to confirm them. This is a case which not unfrequently occurs, and it involves a call "to follow on to know the Lord" (Hosea 6:3).

Or again, we may be in the practice of reading Scripture carefully, and trying to serve God, and its sense may, as if suddenly, break upon us, in a way it never did before. Some thought may suggest itself to us, which is the key to a great deal in Scripture, or which suggests a great many other thoughts. A new light may be thrown on the precepts of our Lord and His Apostles. We may be able to enter into the manner of life of the early Christians, as recorded in Scripture, which before was hidden from us, and into the simple maxims on which Scripture bases it. We may be led to understand that it is very different from the life which [humans] live now. Now knowledge is a call to action: an insight into the way of perfection is a call to perfection. (Newman, *Parochial and Plain Sermons*, VIII, pp. 29–30)

Reflections

Revelation was a source of action for Newman who saw life as a response to a call from God. Knowledge of revelation was the source of activity because revelation demanded not only assent of mind, but also assent of will. Proclamation and response is how we understand Christian worship that has the liturgy of the word followed by the liturgy of the Eucharist.

For Catholics, the Bible has been rediscovered in such a way that its meaning for the whole church and for individuals now speaks louder than it has for centuries. The Bible, rightly understood, changes us as we come to understand it and allow ourselves to be addressed by it. At the same time, biblical scholarship helps Christians avoid biblical literalism and enables them to embrace the proper and restricted realms of science without defensiveness. Newman would appreciate that the Scriptures more readily inform personal spirituality, catechetical teaching, and communal celebration of the sacraments among contemporary Catholics.

✧ In celebrating weddings and funerals, the participants have a wide choice of scripture as part of the planning. What scripture did you choose for a sacramental moment in your life: marriage, funeral, religious vows? Find this scripture and pray over it very slowly this week.

✧ Reviewing this past week, what was the high point of your experience? What was the low point? Open your Bible and find passages that speak to both of these times. Copy them and use them at appropriate times in the week to come.

✧ Spend a week with the lectionary readings. Do not go looking for Scripture passages, but accept what is being read this week by the church in the liturgy. At the end of the week, review your experience: What was hard to accept in the week's readings? What was challenging? What reading made you happiest?

✧ Gather a group to share the Sunday readings ahead of time. Read them quietly and then have someone in the group read them aloud. Listen to each other without judgment. After Sunday worship, reflect on how the sharing made a difference in the quality of your listening and responding at the Eucharist.

✧ Newman seemed "transparent" to a friend who periodically heard him preach. Pray for those who are preparing today to teach or preach the Scriptures. Ask for God's blessing that they may truly serve the word of God.

God's Word

Simeon took him in his arms and praised God, saying,
  "Master, now you are dismissing your servant in
        peace,
    according to your word;
  for my eyes have seen your salvation,
      which you have prepared in the presence of all
        peoples,
  a light for revelation to the Gentiles
      and for glory to your people Israel."

(Luke 2:28–32)

Closing prayer: O God, by your Word you have made all things. Heal our mind and heart by your grace and gospel. May we find ourselves in you, whole and entire, in truth and in love.

✧ Meditation 11 ✧

The Church: One, Holy, Catholic, Apostolic

Theme: Newman's search for God was at the same time a search for the church that was one, holy, catholic, and apostolic.

Opening prayer: God of our fathers and mothers, and God of our children, we believe that the church is the body of Christ and your pilgrim people. Give us a sense of gratitude for the mystery that is your church.

About Newman

Early in 1878, Pope Pius IX died and was succeeded by Leo XIII. Leo was ready to pursue discussions about the relations of the church to the modern world; his later encyclicals show his willingness to tackle the social issues of his day. One of Leo's first decisions was to set in motion the process for awarding the Englishman, John Henry Newman, a figure not always loved in hierarchical circles, the honor of being named a cardinal. In 1879, Newman was received in Rome. The public title of cardinal removed some of the ambiguity around Newman's work. It could now be said that he was acceptable and accepted.

Newman had never been known for making converts; he did not realize until a late date that some in the Roman Catholic communion were expecting exactly that from him. He saw his own work as edification, a building up of the Body of Christ by education and strengthening from within. From his own experience, he said that converts not only have to be ready for the church, the church has to be ready for converts.

Even though he did not seek converts, Newman's whole life had been dedicated to building the whole people of God, the church. His work related to the life of the church: his writings, his preaching, his pastoral work, his educational endeavors. In his early life, Newman had thought that he might be a missionary and was ready to make the sacrifices that living as a missioner would involve. Newman became a kind of champion for the laity. In his Anglican work on Arianism, he recognized that it was the ordinary faithful in the church that had preserved the true faith. In his work on doctrinal development, he highlighted the ecclesial phenomenon of the *sensus fidelium*, or sense of the faithful, the power of the faithful to discern the truth of God and the universal faith of the people of God. It was Newman who spoke of desired characteristics for the laity of his century.

> I want a laity, not arrogant, not rash in speech, not disputatious, but [those] who know their religion, who enter into it, who know just where they stand, who know what they hold, and what they do not, who know their creed so well that they can give an account of it, who know so much of history that they can defend it. I want an intelligent, well-instructed laity. (Henry Tristram, comp., *Living Thoughts of Cardinal Newman*, p. 19)

Newman was always known for speaking straightforwardly and clearly, and up to the end, his message was not always well-received and his motives were sometimes considered suspect. In 1861, he had written:

> There was a class, and ever is a class, whose claims to consideration are too little regarded now, and were passed over then [in Galileo's time]—I mean the educated

class. . . . [Those] who have sharpened their intellects by exercise and study, anticipate the conclusions of the many by some centuries . . . and it is as clear to me that their spiritual state ought to be consulted for, as it is difficult to say why in fact it so often is not. They are to be tenderly regarded for their own sake; they are to be respected and conciliated for the sake of their influence over other classes. I cannot help feeling that, in high circles, the Church is sometimes looked upon as made up of the hierarchy and the poor, and that the educated portion, men and women, are viewed as a difficulty, an encumbrance, as the seat and source of heresy; as almost aliens to the Catholic body, whom it would be a great gain, if possible, to annihilate. (Tristram, comp., *Living Thoughts*, pp. 20–21)

Newman's vision of the church corresponded to the phrase found in the creed of the early centuries: "I believe in one, holy, catholic, and apostolic Church," and in his lifelong search, he thought and wrote about unity, holiness, apostolic teaching, apostolic succession, and catholicity or universality. While he joined the Roman communion, he continued to live believing in "the life of the world to come." Newman, though he did not use the phrase, lived knowing he was a member of the pilgrim church through time.

Pause: Ponder this: Have I ever searched for the church that is one, holy, catholic, and apostolic? What form has that search taken for me?

Newman's Words

In 1848, Newman wrote a novel about a character named Charles Reding, an Anglican who became a Catholic. This passage gives us an idea of Newman's love for the vitality of the church at prayer.

At length the church got very full: rich and poor were mixed together—artisans, well-drest youths, Irish labourers, mothers with two or three children—the only division being that of men from women. . . . Had

Reding continued standing, no one would have noticed him; but he saw the time was come for him to kneel, and accordingly he moved into a corner-seat on the bench nearest him. He had hardly done so, when a procession with lights passed from the sacristy to the altar; something went on which he did not understand, and then suddenly began what, by the *Miserere* and *Ora pro nobis*, he perceived to be a litany; a hymn followed. Reding thought he never had been present at worship before, so absorbed was the attention, so intense was the devotion of the congregation. What particularly struck him was, that whereas in the Church of England the clergyman or the organ was every thing and the people nothing, except so far as the clerk is their representative, here it was just reversed. The priest hardly spoke, or at least audibly; but the whole congregation was as though one vast instrument or Panharmonicon, moving all together, and, what was most remarkable, as if self-moved. They did not seem to require any one to prompt or direct them, though in the Litany the choir took the alternate parts. The words were Latin, but every one seemed to understand them thoroughly, and to be offering up prayers to the Blessed Trinity, and the Incarnate Saviour, and the great Mother of God, and the glorified Saints, with hearts full in proportion to the energy of the sounds they uttered. There was a little boy by him, and a poor woman, singing at the pitch of their voices. There was no mistaking it; Reding said to himself, "This *is* a [religion of the people]." He looked around at the building; it was, as we have said, very plain, and bore the marks of being unfinished; but the Living Temple which was manifested in it needed not curious carving or rich marble to complete it, "for the glory of God did lighten it, and the Lamb was the light thereof." "How wonderful," said Charles to himself, "that people call this worship formal and external; it seems to possess all classes, young and old, polished and vulgar, men and women indiscriminately; it is the working of one Spirit in all, making many one." (Tillotson, comp., *Prose and Poetry*, pp. 348–349)

Reflection

Newman was born into a church that had its own role and relation to political society. However, the church Newman was born into was a union of cross and crown. The episcopal authorities were subordinated to the national government; baptism came as a birthright to the English citizen. As Britain's government became inclusive of people with other religious beliefs or no beliefs at all, the orthodox Anglican party perceived the serious incongruity in this governance structure.

But if the church was not to be subject to the government, where did it get its authority? Why does the church exist? How does the church exist? Newman spent his life dealing with complex questions like these, and his example invites us to think through any church issues that belong to our own time. In his day, as in our own, the church at worship most truly reflects its reason for being and manifests Christ as the saving mystery of God.

Sometimes we might wonder how Newman could give himself to something so limited and tarnished as the Church of Rome. In Matthew, chapter 13, we read that insofar as the church participates in the Reign of God it will be something that reverses our expectations: it is not a cedar of Lebanon, but a mustard bush; it is not, at present, a harvest of saints, but a field of weeds among the wheat; it is not a collection of the pure, but a fishnet hauling in the desirable and the undesirable. And so it will be until the end of time. Newman had both an "unruffled faith in the Catholic Church" and a "conviction of the miserable deficiencies" which existed in it (Dessain, ed., *Letters and Diaries*, XIX, p. 10).

✧ Open your Bible to chapter 13 of Matthew and prayerfully read the chapter. Return to the sections and verses that seem most important to you in your present understanding of the reality of the church. Compose a prayer for the well-being of the church that uses the scriptural images found in Matthew.

✧ If there are older members of the family around, ask them about their church experiences in the past. What was wonderful, sad, funny, or irritating? What has remained a holy memory for them? What changes have they known? Who, in their life, were the uncanonized saints? What did they learn from them? As you listen to their stories, note how their faith comes alive in the recounting of their history.

✧ What is your earliest memory of church? What kind of God did you experience? How have you grown since then? How has the whole church grown since then?

✧ Recall a sacramental experience in which everything seemed to move as one. Evoke in yourself a sense of awe and reverence as you relive this in your imagination. As you move through the rest of the day, continue to awaken this spirit of awe and reverence.

✧ Imagine Newman has come to visit you for the day. Converse with him concerning what he said about the laity. Share your own thoughts with him. Write your own description of the kind of laity the church needs today.

✧ Do you know what your mission in life is? If so, reflect on the growth and fluctuations you have known within that mission. If not, sit with a friend and discuss your strongest and weakest talents, your desires and fears, and the needs you perceive in your present surroundings. For a selected period of time, pray each day for missionaries, and unite your intentions with theirs.

✧ Bishops get letters of complaint and suggestion, but perhaps not enough positive letters. Is there something positive you could write about to your bishop? If you speak to your parish liturgical committee, perhaps you could find a way to personalize the prayer at the Eucharist for your bishop.

✧ The strength of the early church was in the small groups. If you belong to a small faith group, spend time praying for each person. Compose a prayer that is reflective of the needs and spirit of the whole group. If you do not belong to a small faith group, ask for the guidance of the Holy Spirit in discerning if you should begin one.

God's Word

I, therefore, the prisoner in the Lord, beg you to lead a life worthy of the calling to which you have been called, with all humility and gentleness, with patience, bearing with one another in love, making every effort to maintain the unity of the Spirit in the bond of peace. (Ephesians 4:1–3)

Closing prayer:

O God, may I receive the gift of perseverance in grace, and die as I have desired to live, in your faith, in your church, in your service, and in your love. (Adapted from *Meditations and Devotions*, p. 290)

✧ Meditation 12 ✧

Mary, the Mother of God

Theme: Reverence toward Mary, the mother of God, grew in Newman along with his commitment to the mystery of God in Christ.

Opening prayer: Hail Mary, full of grace, the Lord is with you.

About Newman

When Newman was reading the Fathers of the Church, mainly Athanasius, he came to an important insight about his faith at the time: he was a Monophysite. A Monophysite believed Christ had one nature, a divine nature. In time, the Council of Chalcedon declared that there were two natures in Christ, a divine nature and a human nature. When Newman concluded that he was a Monophysite, he began to consider more seriously the implications of the human nature of Christ, and the figure of Mary moved to the forefront of his attention in a new way.

Newman wrote that it was Saint Athanasius who first brought the circumstances of the Incarnation home to human minds and "engraved indelibly upon the imaginations of the faithful, as had never been before, that man is God, and God is man, that in Mary they meet, and that in this sense Mary is the centre of all things" (Newman, *Difficulties Felt by Anglicans*, II, p. 87).

Newman's love of and familiarity with the Scriptures interacted with his love and understanding of the apostolic teaching that was formulated in the creeds of the early Christians. Newman himself loved using his senses in the world around him; he enjoyed the engagement with sympathetic and like-minded friends. These things fed his imagination and intellect, and it is this approach that took shape in his devotion to and teaching about the human and divine Jesus and his mother, Mary.

When Newman became an Oratorian, and responsible for the houses both in London and in Birmingham, trouble arose. The Brompton house in London, under the direction of Faber,

> accepted with alacrity all sentimentalities and exaggerations of Italian devotion, which Newman considered quite suitable for southern temperaments, but repugnant to the English character. The London Oratorians would call the Blessed Virgin their dear "Mama" and use a host of "little" devotions of all kinds; they were much opposed to intellectual activity which they considered unspiritual. (Hilda Graef, *God and Myself*, p. 133)

Newman found these devotions, when they were written for imitation, as "repulsive as love-letters in a police report" (Newman, *Difficulties Felt by Anglicans*, II, p. 80). His study and readings had given the emotions of his heart another grounding. The Marian liturgical feasts, the writings of the early church, and the rosary and the litany of Mary were sufficient riches for him.

Pause: Have I ever turned to or away from Mary in my life of faith? Why?

Newman's Words

Newman wrote these words as an introduction to meditations on the titles used for Mary in her litany:

> Why is May chosen as the month in which we exercise a special devotion to the Blessed Virgin? The first reason

is because it is the time when the earth bursts forth into its fresh foliage and its green grass after the stern frost and snow of winter, and the raw atmosphere and the wild wind and rain of the early spring. It is because the blossoms are upon the trees and the flowers are in the gardens. It is because the days have got long, and the sun rises early and sets late. For such gladness and joyousness of external Nature is a fit attendant on our devotion to her who is the Mystical Rose and the House of Gold.

[Someone] may say, "True; but in this climate we have sometimes a bleak, inclement May." This cannot be denied; but still, so much is true that at least it is the month of *promise* and of *hope*. Even though the weather happen to be bad, it is the month that *begins* and heralds in the summer. We know, for all that may be unpleasant in it, that fine weather is coming, sooner or later. "Brightness and beautifulness shall," in the Prophet's words, "appear at the end, and shall not lie: if it make delay, wait for it, for it shall surely come, and shall not be slack."

May then is the month, if not of fulfillment, at least of *promise*; and is not this the very aspect in which we most suitably regard the Blessed Virgin, Holy Mary, to whom this month is dedicated?

The Prophet says, "There shall come forth a rod out of the root of Jesse, and a flower shall rise out of his root." Who is the flower but our Blessed Lord? Who is the rod, or beautiful stalk or stem or plant out of which the flower grows, but Mary, Mother of our Lord, Mary, Mother of God?

It was prophesied that God should come upon earth. When the time was now full, how was it announced? It was announced by the Angel coming to Mary. "Hail, full of grace" said Gabriel, "the Lord is with thee; blessed art thou among women." She then was the sure *promise* of the coming Saviour, and therefore May is by a special title her month. (*Meditations and Devotions*, pp. 3–4)

Reflection

Mary is a powerful figure in Christianity, scripturally as the mother of Jesus and doctrinally as the mother of the Incarnate Word. Newman's devotion to Mary grew as he moved on in his own intellectual, moral, and religious journey of faith. He was aware that national temperaments and individual differences existed that would lead the members of the church to express their devotion to Mary and to the saints differently. His concern was only that the acts of devotion be fitting and that they be consonant with doctrinal teaching. For himself, he said, "I prefer English habits of belief and devotion to foreign, from the same causes, and by the same right, which justifies foreigners in preferring their own" (Newman, *Difficulties Felt by Anglicans*, II, p. 20). At bottom though, Newman had a profound appreciation of and devotion to Mary as "the sure promise of the coming Saviour" who was human and divine.

✧ One of Newman's preferred devotions was saying the rosary. Take time, in a quiet place at home, in a garden, or on a walk, to say the rosary.

✧ Each evening in the Anglican, Catholic, and Orthodox services, the canticle of Mary is prayed. It is found in Luke 1:46–55. For some evenings, pray this ancient prayer. Why do you think it was chosen for the evening? Are you able to say that you proclaim the greatness of God, that your spirit rejoices in God as Savior?

✧ The second of February is the feast day celebrating the presentation of Jesus in the Temple. The Gospel of the day includes Luke 2:29–32, Simeon's canticle that is used every night for night prayer in the liturgy of the hours. In the following verses, Simeon says to Mary, "and a sword will pierce your own soul too" (Luke 2:35). How is Mary like so many mothers in the world who suffer with the sufferings of their children? What place could Mary hold for you in your confrontation with suffering?

✧ Luke's Gospel says Jesus was obedient to Mary and Joseph in Nazareth. His mother kept the mysterious event of the finding of Jesus, the runaway, in the Temple as something to ponder in her heart (Luke 2:51). What have you pondered in your heart as you lived in your family? When did you or members of your family have to assert autonomy so that you or they could later love and act as whole people? Could you spend some time talking with a group of young people and praying with them?

✧ Pray the following litany, an excerpt of a litany known and prayed by Newman, with the response, Pray for us. When you are finished, compose your own prayer.

> Mary, Mother of the Living God,
> Mary, Daughter of the Light Unapproachable,
> Mary, our light,
> Mary, our sister,
> Mary, stem of Jesse,
> Mary, offspring of kings,
> Mary, best work of God,
> Mary, immaculate,
> Mary, all fair,
> Mary, Virgin Mother,
> Mary, suffering with Jesus,
> Mary, pierced with a sword,
> Mary, bereft of consolation,
> Mary, standing by the Cross,
> Mary, ocean of bitterness,
> Mary, rejoicing in God's will,
> Mary, our Lady,
> Mary, our Queen,
> Mary, bright as the sun,
> Mary, fair as the moon,
> Mary, crowned with twelve stars,
> Mary, seated at the right hand of Jesus,
> Mary, our sweetness,
> Mary, our hope,
> Mary, glory of Jerusalem,
> Mary, joy of Israel,
> Mary, honour of our people
>   (*Meditations and Devotions*, pp. 244–245)

✧ Read the "God's Word" section on the following page. To whom are you being sent now?

God's Word

In those days Mary set out and went with haste to a Judean town in the hill country, where she entered the house of Zechariah and greeted Elizabeth. When Elizabeth heard Mary's greeting, the child leaped in her womb. And Elizabeth was filled with the Holy Spirit and exclaimed with a loud cry, "Blessed are you among women, and blessed is the fruit of your womb. And why has this happened to me, that the mother of my Lord comes to me? For as soon as I heard the sound of your greeting, the child in my womb leaped for joy. And blessed is she who believed that there would be a fulfillment of what was spoken to her by the Lord." (Luke 1:39–45)

Closing prayer:

The freshness of May,
    and the sweetness of June,
And the fire of July
    in its passionate noon,
Munificent August,
    September serene,
Are together no match
    for my glorious Queen.

O Mary, all months
    and all days are thine own,
In thee lasts their joyousness,
    when they are gone;
And we give to thee May,
    not because it is best,
But because it comes first,
    and is pledge of the rest.

(Tillotson, comp., *Prose and Poetry*, pp. 811–812)

✧ Meditation 13 ✧

Music and Poetry

Theme: Newman's active life also included music and poetry as expressions of his thoughts and the feelings of his heart.

Opening prayer:

Praise to you, Yahweh, in your sanctuary! . . .
Praise with timbrel and dance;
Praise with strings and flute.

(Psalm 150:1,4)

About Newman

In his later years, Newman and two old Anglican friends reconciled. As a token of their restored friendship, the two old friends sent Newman the gift of a fine violin. Newman's thank-you is charming and perceptive in an offhand way:

> I really think [the violin] will add to my power of working, and the length of my life. I never wrote more than when I played the fiddle. I always sleep better after music. There must be some electric current passing from the strings through the fingers into the brain and down the spinal marrow. Perhaps thought is music. (Dessain, ed., *Letters and Diaries*, XXII, p. 9)

"Perhaps thought is music." Words alone will not evoke or express the wholeness of the mystery of life. Throughout his lifetime, Newman believed that moving from the adoration of God, a real apprehension of the divine mystery, into words of theology and creedal statements, a notional apprehension, was a woeful necessity. He cautioned against the profanation of the sacred mysteries by an idolatry of language.

When human language is needed to express or evoke sacred mysteries, Newman preferred both music and poetry. In 1865, Newman became famous for his long poem, "The Dream of Gerontius," which recounts in verse form the transition to eternal life through the passage of death.

Newman's attraction to Catholicism and aversion to the Protestantism of his day was reflected in his deep personal response to the church's liturgy and personalized mode of religious instruction. For Newman, the church's very being is poetry.

> [The church] is the poet of . . . children; full of music to soothe the sad and control the wayward,—wonderful in story for the imagination of the romantic; rich in symbol and imagery, so that gentle and delicate feelings, which will not bear words, may in silence intimate their presence or commune with themselves. (John Henry Cardinal Newman, *Essays Critical and Historical*, II, pp. 442–443)

Music and art, Newman believed, were particularly congenial to the spirit of Saint Philip and Oratorian spirituality. These creative arts were always employed in their ministerial works and in the liturgy of the word.

Pause: Ask yourself, What role do music, art, and poetry play in my life of faith?

Newman's Words

In *Loss and Gain*, Newman's novel about the conversion of an Oxford student, Charles Reding, he describes the young man:

> Without being himself a poet, he was in the season of poetry, in the sweet spring-time, when the year is most

beautiful, because it is new. Novelty was beauty to a heart so open and cheerful as his, not only because it was novelty, and had its proper charm as such, but because when we first see things, we see them in a "gay confusion," which is a principal element of the poetical. As time goes on, and we number and sort and measure things—as we gain views—we advance towards philosophy and truth, but we recede from poetry." (Pp. 18–19)

Reflection

In poetry and music, Newman was not trying to replace thinking with feeling. He was trying to assert the reality that thinking tries to capture in another way. Poetry and music allow realities to capture us. Newman did not believe it possible for anyone to be a theologian without having been grasped personally by the reality of God. Theology tries to put into a system that reality of being grasped by God. However, many people cannot think about God in a systematic way, but all people can be grasped by God. When this happens, music and poetry are common ways to express the experience.

✧ Newman especially liked the works of Beethoven. Take time yourself to listen quietly and attentively to one of Beethoven's works. Compose your own melody or prayer of thanksgiving when you are finished listening to the music.

✧ Find a favorite song or poem. Enjoy it again, reflecting on the movement of your feelings within you and the thoughts you have. How does this song or poem affect faith or hope or love in your life?

✧ Find a book of poems and use them for meditation. Let the words from a selected few awaken and express what is deep within you. Close with a prayer that the gift of poetry may flourish.

✧ Look in your church hymnal and find a hymn that you especially like for your parish community. Hum it, or sing it to yourself, imagining the whole parish community humming or singing with you. How does this hymn reflect the life or needs of your parish church? Spend some time praying for your church's musical community, asking for the grace to worship well.

✧ If it is possible, attend an Eastern rite service or a worship service with a gospel choir. Enter into the recitations, the singing, and the movements of this community of praise.

✧ Ask yourself: Is there any resolution I should make about daily praising through music and poetry? If so, take time to write your resolution.

God's Word

Be filled with the Spirit, as you sing psalms and hymns and spiritual songs among yourselves, singing and making melody to [God] in your hearts, giving thanks to God . . . at all times and for everything in the name of . . . Jesus Christ. (Ephesians 5:18–20)

Closing prayer:

Sing to Yahweh a new song of praise
in the assembly of the faithful.
Let Israel rejoice in their Maker;
Let the people of Zion be glad in their God.
Let them praise God's name in a festive dance;
let them sing praise to God with timbrel and harp.
For God loves the people
and crowns the lowly with victory.

(Psalm 149:1–4)

✧ Meditation 14 ✧

Death and Dying

Theme: Experiencing and confronting the death of those we love is a great challenge to faith and hope. Throughout the decades of his life, Newman suffered the losses of death.

Opening prayer: Into your hands, Almighty God, we commend ourselves and all those we have loved.

About Newman

By temperament, Newman was very attached to those who had endeared themselves to him, either as members of his family or as friends. Thus, their deaths, at whatever their age and whatever Newman's age, were a cause of great grief and suffering to him.

In January 1828, John Henry was not quite twenty-seven years old and his youngest sister, Mary, was just nineteen. She became ill one evening at the supper table, had a bad night, and died the next day. Of her, Newman writes, "I thought I loved her too well, and hardly ever dared to take my full swing of enjoyment in her dear society." (Tristram, ed., *Autobiographical Writings*, p. 213)

In the spring after she died, Newman wrote to another sister about the nagging feeling of loss of his sister Mary:

The country too is beautiful—the fresh leaves, the scents, the varied landscape. Yet I never felt so intensely the transitory nature of this world as when most delighted with these country scenes. . . . I wish it were possible for words to put down those indefinite vague and withal subtle feelings which quite pierce the soul and make it sick. Dear Mary seems embodied in every tree and hid behind every hill. What a veil and curtain this world of sense is! Beautiful, but still a veil. (Ker and Gornall, eds., *Letters and Diaries*, II, p. 69)

Newman here expresses the pain of loss, the elusive search, the sense of living in two worlds, not sure which is more real. This death was one of the first that changed Newman's familiar world.

Six years later, Newman's closest Oxford friend, Hurrell Froude, died. Two years younger than Newman and born into a traditional High Church Anglican family, Froude was witty and sociable. He nevertheless practiced a hidden asceticism and had a serious prayer life. Contact with Froude changed Newman profoundly; he especially profited by Froude's estimation of celibacy. He was definitely High Church for the evangelical Newman. Froude prayed the liturgy of the hours from the breviary; he enjoyed thinking about saints. He had great devotion to the Blessed Virgin. These interests, coupled with a happy and playful personality, were a witness to Newman of what Anglo-Catholicism could be. At Froude's death, Newman wrote, "I feel the longer I live, the more I shall miss him" (Thomas Gornall, ed., *Letters and Diaries of John Henry Cardinal Newman*, V, p. 263). He also realized with poignancy that in time, memories of his friend would fade, and his image would become fainter and fainter. Death made his friend irretrievable.

The last year of Newman's life as an Anglican, 1844, was also the year John William Bowden died. Bowden was a close friend from undergraduate days at Trinity College, and Newman had stayed with him and his wife whenever he was in London. Bowden died in the middle of Newman's crisis of faith in regard to the Church of England. In his autobiography, Newman was not ashamed to admit that "I sobbed bitterly over his coffin, to think that he left me still dark as to what the way of truth was, and what I ought to do in order to please

God and fulfill His will" (*Apologia*, p. 227). With Bowden's death, Newman experienced the frustration of death, the sense of unfinished business, and the loss of advice and companionship that he had expected his friend to continue to give him. Death changed Newman's expectations.

Thirty years later, Newman's longtime friend died. Ambrose St. John had come into full communion in the Roman Catholic church with Newman, went to Rome for studies with him, and remained with him in the Birmingham Oratory when all the other original members had died or left. He passed away a few days before the feast of Saint Philip Neri in May 1875. This time Newman was calm, despite stories to the contrary. But this loss, Newman said, "is the greatest [affliction] I have had in my life" (Charles S. Dessain and Thomas Gornall, eds., *Letters and Diaries of John Henry Cardinal Newman*, XXVII, p. 313). While Ambrose was still alive, Newman wrote in his autobiography these famous lines of dedication:

> And to you especially, dear Ambrose St. John; whom God gave me, when He took every one else away; who are the link between my old life and my new; who have now for twenty-one years been so devoted to me, so patient, so zealous, so tender; who have let me lean so hard upon you; who have watched me so narrowly; who have never thought of yourself, if I was in question." (*Apologia*, p. 283)

Perhaps Newman was calmest at his greatest loss because he had shared so much of his soul and his life with St. John, and he himself was an aged man. When Newman died fifteen years later, he was buried in the same grave as his friend.

Pause: How has the death of others affected my life? How has it affected my faith, my hope, my love?

Newman's Words

Ten years before the death of Ambrose St. John, Newman wrote his famous poem, "The Dream of Gerontius," which has as its theme the death of a Christian. This is the prayer of the priest as Gerontius dies:

Proficiscere, anima Christiana, de hoc mundo!
Go forth upon thy journey, Christian soul!
Go from this world! Go, in the name of God
The Omnipotent Father, who created thee!
Go, in the Name of Jesus Christ, our Lord,
Son of the living God, who bled for thee!
Go, in the Name of the Holy Spirit, who
Hath been pour'd out on thee! Go, in the name
Of Angels and Archangels; in the name
Of Thrones and Dominations; in the name
Of Princedoms and of Powers; and in the name
Of Cherubim and Seraphim, go forth!
Go, in the name of Patriarchs and Prophets;
And of Apostles and Evangelists,
Of Martyrs and Confessors; in the name
Of holy Monks and Hermits; in the name
Of Holy Virgins; and all Saints of God,
Both men and women, go! Go on thy course;
And may thy place to-day be found in peace,
And may thy dwelling be the Holy Mount
Of Sion:—through the Same, through Christ, our Lord.
(John Henry Cardinal Newman, *Verses on Various Occasions*, pp. 330–331)

Reflection

Newman's responses to death reflect our shared humanity. Upon announcement, we are often stunned, sick, tearful, bereft. Gradually we begin to assimilate the meaning of the loss. This may mean a deeper pain, an anger at our friends for dying and leaving us without them. We may find ourselves looking for them in familiar places, hoping to have some sign of their presence. In our sorrow we may become sullen, impatient, frustrated, or deeply disappointed. Hopefully, we will begin to appreciate who each person was in our life, to take to ourselves some of their good characteristics, to engage ourselves in the work and mission that motivated them, and to arrive at a peaceful acceptance of and an acquiescence to the mystery of death, a mystery which has been assumed in Christ.

✧ Before Newman's own death, he let his wishes be known concerning his burial spot. He chose a motto to be engraved on his memorial tablet. He wrote his last letter, inviting his niece, Grace Langford, the daughter of his estranged sister Harriet, for a visit. He died a few days after her visit. Newman models for us the preparation for our own death. Think of someone you know, for whom it would be appropriate to do end of life preparation. Is there some way you can help him or her to do that?

✧ Reread the last stanza of "The Pillar of the Cloud." Reflect on your own journey, the smiling faces you have loved, the losses you have known.

✧ The epitaph on Newman's memorial tablet, which he wrote himself, says, *"Ex Umbris et Imaginibus in Veritatem"*—"Out of the shadows and images into the truth." What motto would you choose for your headstone? Why?

✧ Get a copy of the official prayers for the dying. Say these slowly for everyone who is dying this day. Journal about your thoughts and feelings.

✧ Plan your wake and funeral using the new rite now in effect. Study it carefully and look especially at the options for readings and music. The rite includes a place for a song of farewell as the body is blessed. What choice would you make there? Why? If you wish, write out your choices and reflections and keep them in an appropriate place.

✧ Think of four significant people in your life who have died. Create a litany naming four characteristics for each one that you wish you could have in your own life. Say this litany during the in-between times of the day.

✧ How do you remember those who have died? Do you remember the anniversary of their death? Newman kept the anniversaries of his friends' deaths all his life. We have All Souls Day and Memorial Day for remembering everyone at once. What customs for remembering those who have died have meant the most for you?

God's Word

When Jesus saw [Lazarus' sister] weeping, and the Jews who came with her also weeping, he was greatly disturbed in spirit and deeply moved. He said, "Where have you laid him?" They said to him, "Lord, come and see." Jesus began to weep.

[Jesus] cried with a loud voice, "Lazarus, come out!" The dead man came out, his hands and feet bound with strips of cloth, and his face wrapped in a cloth. Jesus said to them, "Unbind him, and let him go." (John 11:33–35, 43–44)

Closing prayer: May the love of God and the peace of our Savior bless us and console us, gently wipe away every tear from our eyes, and bring us to everlasting life.

✧ Meditation 15 ✧

Faith and Action

Theme: Newman believed that it was not knowledge but faith that provided the impetus for action. Religion, not knowledge, is what gives vigor to the moral life within the human heart and within human society.

Opening prayer: God of life, let me love you in deed as well as in thought so that all you have given to me may bring life to others.

About Newman

There was a movement in Newman's day to do away with religious controversy, and to promote a harmonious and peaceful society by means of literature, science, and cultural events. It was believed that improved knowledge would be a unifying force in society.

In 1841, Newman wrote a series of letters to the *Times* in London which were later put together in pamphlet form and entitled the *Tamworth Reading Room*. He satirizes the role given to the reading room and the place its founders gave to secular knowledge. Newman makes the point that knowledge is one thing, the ability to act rightly is another.

> To know is one thing; to do is another; the two things are altogether distinct. A man knows he should get up in the morning—he lies a-bed; he knows he should not lose his temper, yet he cannot keep it. A labouring man knows he should not go to the ale-house, and his wife knows she should not filch when she goes out charing; but, nevertheless, in these cases, the consciousness of a duty is not all one with the performance of it. (Tillotson, comp., *Prose and Poetry*, pp. 80–81)

He also notes that diversionary pursuits are given as a means of preserving tranquillity.

> When a husband is gloomy, or an old woman peevish and fretful, those who are about them do all they can to keep dangerous topics and causes of offence out of the way, and think themselves lucky, if, by such skillful management, they get through the day without an outbreak. . . . If a man was in grief, he was to be amused; if disappointed, to be excited; if in a rage, to be soothed; if in love, to be roused to the pursuit of glory. No inward change was contemplated, but a change of external objects. (Tillotson, comp., *Prose and Poetry*, p. 82)

Newman, not surprisingly, believes that a moral life is not just impulse and emotion, but a reality having its own laws consisting of habits and capable of direction and refinement from within.

Newman also addresses the griefs involved in living and the desires of the human heart. Satirically he says that the devotees of the reading room believe that intellectual activity and scientific pursuits will make the heart forget its grief for a time. After that, those in grief can resort to digestive pills before dinner, hot milk at bedtime, even "dram-drinking and opium." Newman, of course, does not concur. "Strong liquors, indeed, do for a time succeed in their object; but who was ever consoled in real trouble by the small beer of literature or science?" (Tillotson, comp., *Prose and Poetry*, pp. 83–84).

Newman writes, "If virtue be a mastery over the mind, if its end be action, if its perfection be inward order, harmony, and peace, we must seek it in graver and holier places than in Libraries and Reading Rooms" (Tillotson, comp., *Prose and Poetry*, p. 85).

Pause: Consider: What role does knowledge play in my life? What really motivates me to action? Where do I turn for consolation in the face of grief?

Newman's Words

Glory, science, knowledge, and whatever other fine names we use, never healed a wounded heart, nor changed a sinful one; but the Divine Word is with power. The ideas which Christianity brings before us are in themselves full of influence, and they are attended with a supernatural gift over and above themselves, in order to meet the special exigencies of our nature. Knowledge is not "power," nor is glory "the first and only fair"; but "Grace," or the "Word," by whichever name we call it, has been from the first a quickening, renovating, organizing principle. It has new created the individual, and transferred and knit [the individual] into a social body, composed of members each similarly created. It has cleansed man of his moral diseases, raised him to hope and energy, given him to propagate a brotherhood among his fellows, and to found a family or rather a kingdom of saints all over the earth;—it introduced a new force into the world, and the impulse which it gave continues in its original vigour down to this day. Each one of us has lit his lamp from his neighbour, or received it from fathers, and the lights thus transmitted are at this time as strong and as clear as if 1800 years had not passed since the kindling of the sacred flame. What has glory or knowledge been able to do like this? (Tillotson, comp., *Prose and Poetry*, p. 86)

Reflection

Newman as a young intellectual and a scholar set no value on knowledge as some kind of virtue. He could value knowledge for knowledge's sake, but he did not consider intellectuals, by their education, to be elevated above others or morally better than others.

But other Victorians had great faith in the moral power of education by itself. When the English politician Robert Peel came to the town of Tamworth to dedicate a public reading room, he proclaimed his belief that education could, in effect, be a substitute for religion, and that the reading room, if well-utilized, would promote public virtue and social cohesion. Where religion had promoted ignorance and superstition, knowledge would humanize and elevate. Where religion had promoted controversy and division by insisting on dogma, knowledge would unify through experiment and science. The study of the natural arts and sciences would heal and unite. Newman thought this absurd.

Newman countered that secular knowledge was neither a principle, a means, nor an antecedent to moral improvement. Further, secular knowledge was neither a principle of social unity nor a principle of action. In the main, Newman totally disagreed with Peel. However, Newman did not contest the desirability of knowledge; he did not consider science "infidelity"; he acknowledged a place for both utility and amusement in human affairs. But for Newman, faith came first, and faith was the principle, not only for moral improvement, but for social unity and action.

✧ Write down five things that mean the most to you in your faith at this time. Next to each one, write your age when this particular belief came home to you and you took it to heart. Next, write down when and from whom you first heard the idea. Meditate on what was happening from the time you first heard the idea to the time when it truly entered your heart.

✧ Read the "About Newman" section again. Examine yourself using the following questions:
✦ Do I ever find myself not doing what I know I should do?
✦ Do I ever find myself appeasing others or making others appease me in order to keep a situation harmonious?
✦ Do I ever find myself using diversions or external medications to avoid dealing with my real responsibilities or my cares?

✧ Build a fire in a fireplace or light a candle. Reflect on those who have enlightened your life and passed on the living flame of religion to you. Dwell silently in the presence of the flame.

✧ Think of those to whom you are responsible for handing on the faith. Pray the prayer said at the baptism of children:

Parents and godparents, this light is entrusted to you to be kept burning brightly. [These children of yours have] been enlightened by Christ. [They are] to walk always as [children] of the light. May [they] keep the flame of faith alive in [their] heart. When the Lord comes, may [they] go out to meet him with all the saints in the heavenly kingdom. (*Rites of the Catholic Church*, I, p. 404)

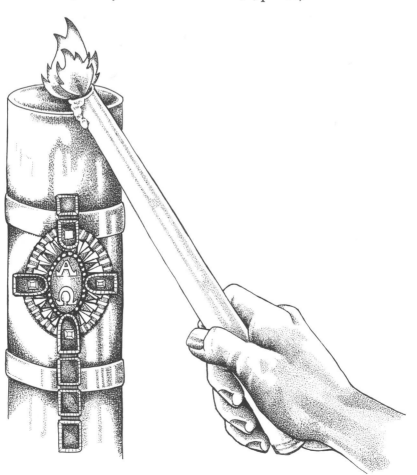

✧ Have you ever bought something "useful" or "entertaining," but then hardly ever used it after the initial enthusiasm wore off? What happened? What were you looking for? What did you learn about needing change in your life? Do you still have this object? Can it be used again or should it be given away to help other people?

✧ What calls to action have you overlooked in your life? Are there many or is there a central one you have not responded to? When the call of "Lord have mercy, Christ have mercy" comes in the liturgy, ask God for assistance in this.

God's Word

When he came to Nazareth, where he had been brought up, [Jesus] went to the synagogue on the sabbath day, as was his custom. He stood up to read, and the scroll of the prophet Isaiah was given to him. He unrolled the scroll and found the place where it was written:
"The Spirit of the Lord is upon me,
because he has anointed me
to bring good news to the poor.
He has sent me to proclaim release to the captives
and recovery of sight to the blind,
to let the oppressed go free,
to proclaim the year of [God's] favor."

(Luke 4:16–19)

Closing prayer:

[Your name], you have been enlightened by Christ.
Walk always as a child of light
and keep the flame of faith alive in your heart.

C·O·M·M·U·N·I·O·N

✧ **For Further Reading** ✧

Chadwick, Owen. *Newman.* New York: Oxford University Press, 1983.

Bouyer, Louis. *Newman.* New York: Meridian Books, 1960.

Dessain, C. S. *The Spirituality of John Henry Newman.* Minneapolis: Winston Press, 1977.

Elwood, J. Murray. *Kindly Light: The Spiritual Vision of John Henry Newman.* Notre Dame, IN: Ave Maria Press, 1979.

Ker, Ian. *Newman: On Being a Christian.* Notre Dame, IN: University of Notre Dame Press, 1990.

Sugg, Joyce, ed. *A Packet of Letters.* Oxford, England: Clarendon Press, 1983.

Trevor, Meriol. *Newman's Journey.* Huntington, IN: Our Sunday Visitor Press, 1985.

Acknowledgments *(continued)*

The psalms in this book are from *Psalms Anew: In Inclusive Language,* compiled by Nancy Schreck and Maureen Leach (Winona, MN: Saint Mary's Press, 1986). Copyright © 1986 by Saint Mary's Press. All rights reserved.

All other scriptural quotations in this book are from the New Revised Standard Version of the Bible. Copyright © 1989 by the Division of Christian Education of the National Council of the Churches of Christ in the United States of America. All rights reserved.

The excerpts on pages 14, 20, 73–74, 74, 75 (first excerpt), and 75 (second excerpt) are from *Young Mr. Newman,* by Maisie Ward (New York: Sheed and Ward, 1948), pages 19, 249, 9–10, 362–363, 363, and 401, respectively. Copyright © 1948 by Sheed and Ward. Reprinted by permission of Sheed and Ward, 115 E. Armour Blvd., Kansas City, MO 64141, 800-333-7373.

The excerpt on page 15 is from *Discussions and Arguments on Various Subjects,* by John Henry Cardinal Newman (London: Longmans, Green, and Company, 1899), page 293.

The excerpts on pages 16, 48, 63–64, and 103–104 are from *The Letters and Diaries of John Henry Newman,* edited by Ian Ker and Thomas Gornall, SJ (Oxford, England: Clarendon Press, 1979), pages 58 (vol. II), 51 and 54–55 (vol. XII), 447–448 (vol. XVII), and 69 (vol. II), respectively. Copyright © 1979 by the Birmingham Oratory. Used by permission of Oxford University Press.

The excerpts on pages 19, 39, 62, 87–88, 98, 111 (first excerpt), 111 (second excerpt), 111 (third excerpt), 111 (fourth excerpt), and 112 are from *Newman: Prose and Poetry,* compiled by Geoffrey Tillotson (Cambridge, MA: Harvard University Press, 1965), pages 807, 807, 831, 348–349, 811–812, 80–81, 82, 83–84, 85, and 86, respectively.

The excerpt on page 21 is from *Newman: The Pillar of the Cloud,* by Meriol Trevor (Garden City, NY: Doubleday and Company, 1962), page 252. Copyright © 1962 by Meriol Trevor.

The excerpts on pages 23, 26–27, 31–32, 32 (first excerpt), 32 (second excerpt), 37–38, 59, 104–105, and 105 are from *Apologia Pro Vita Sua,* by John Henry Cardinal Newman (London: Longmans, Green, and Company, 1897), pages 238, 266–268, 4–5, 3–4, 6–7, 29, 24, 227, and 283, respectively. Copyright © 1969 by Clarendon Press.

The excerpt on page 26 is from *Arians of the Fourth Century,* by John Henry Cardinal Newman (London: Longmans, Green, and Company, 1897), page 445.

The excerpts on pages 27, 70 (first excerpt), 70 (second excerpt), 70 (third excerpt), 71, 92, 93, and 95 are from *Certain Difficulties Felt*

The excerpts on pages 64 and 103 are from *John Henry Newman: Autobiographical Writings*, edited by Henry Tristram (New York: Sheed and Ward, 1957), pages 254 and 213. Copyright © 1957 by Sheed and Ward.

The excerpt on pages 68–69 is from *John Henry Newman: A Biography*, by Ian Ker (Oxford, England: Oxford University Press, 1988), page 284. Copyright © 1988 by Ian Ker. Used by permission of Oxford University Press.

The excerpts on pages 75–76, 76–77, and 77 are from *A Packet of Letters*, edited by Joyce Sugg (Oxford, England: Clarendon Press, 1983), pages 116–117, 199–200, and 141, respectively. Copyright © 1983 by the Birmingham Oratory. Used by permission of Oxford University Press.

The excerpts on pages 80–81 and 81 are from *Letters and Correspondence of John Henry Newman*, vol. II, edited by Anne Mozley (London: Longmans, Green, and Company, 1890), pages 442 and 383.

The excerpts on pages 86 and 86–87 are from *The Living Thoughts of Cardinal Newman*, compiled by Henry Tristram (London: Cassell and Company, 1948), pages 19 and 20–21.

The excerpt on page 93 is from *God and Myself*, by Hilda Graef (New York: Hawthorn Books, 1968), page 133. Copyright © 1968 by Hilda Graef.

The excerpt on page 100 is from *Essays Critical and Historical*, vol. II, by John Henry Cardinal Newman (London: Longmans, Green, and Company, 1897), pages 442–443.

The excerpt on pages 100–101 is from *Loss and Gain*, by John Henry Cardinal Newman (London: Longmans, Green, and Company, 1898), pages 18–19.

The excerpt on page 104 is from *The Letters and Diaries of John Henry Newman*, vol. V, edited by Thomas Gornall, SJ (Oxford, England: Clarendon Press, 1981), page 263. Copyright © 1981 by the Birmingham Oratory.

The excerpt on page 105 is from *The Letters and Diaries of John Henry Newman*, vol. XXVII, edited by Charles S. Dessain and Thomas Gornall, SJ (Oxford, England: Clarendon Press, 1975), page 313. Copyright © 1975 by the Birmingham Oratory.

The excerpt on page 106 is from *Verses on Various Occasions*, by John Henry Cardinal Newman (London: Longmans, Green, and Company, 1903), pages 330–331.

The excerpt on page 114 is from *Rites of the Catholic Church*, vol. I, an English translation of the "Rite of Baptism for Children" (New York: Pueblo Publishing Company, 1990), page 404. Copyright © 1990 by Pueblo Publishing Company.

Titles in the Companions for the Journey Series